CW00410417

What People Are Saying About
Courts of Law Not Courts of Justice

"*Courts of Law Not Courts of Justice*, rather than picking a side, reveals dark aspects of our criminal justice system when viewed from a variety of angles. Highly engaging, thought-provoking, and easy to read, Mr. Oberer has provided us with an exposé worthy of the read."
—Patrick Daly, Former Maryland Assistant Attorney General & Maryland Assistant State's Attorney

"I've known Eric since we were children, the time when we became friends. We remain friends in adulthood. He has always been a person who has lived his life with integrity and strong moral principles. He has always had many concerns about the hardships that others have faced and wanted to help change the conditions of all people, especially those individuals that live in poverty-ridden areas. As someone who spent large portions of his childhood in high-crime White areas as well as high-crime African-American areas, in addition to having been a guns, drugs, and violent crimes prosecutor in Baltimore, I believe that Eric is uniquely situated to provide keen insights into the American justice system. As the Principal of an inner-city charter school for at-risk youth, each day, I see firsthand the impact that the justice system has on society and the significance of the perceptions and realities of the justice system on the lives of many. *Courts of Law Not Courts of Justice* provides an inside look at how the justice system operates in America and ought to be considered required reading for anyone that wants to know how things work."
—Terrell S. Williams, Principal, Riverscape Career Tech High School

"Eric Oberer boils down complex legal rulings and theories in a thorough yet understandable manner. His descriptions of these fundamental American rights help the reader to appreciate the many legal and political issues in the news today. *Courts of Law Not Courts of Justice* is a valuable tool for understanding the issues of our day and the events that led to them."
—Michael N. Russo, Jr., Partner, Council, Baradel, Kosmerl & Nolan, P.A.

"*Courts of Law Not Courts of Justice* should be a required text for all law students but will easily be enjoyed by all readers interested in our system of justice. The book presents an incredibly articulate and cogent critique of the American criminal justice system. Mr. Oberer's work provides the historical context for understanding how well-intended political policies dealing with crime coupled with inadequate public resources can result in the inconsistent and deficient dispensation of justice throughout our legal system."

—J. Paul Rieger, Jr., Attorney and American Author

"*Courts of Law Not Courts of Justice* is necessary reading for anyone concerned with the urban criminal justice system or affected by it. This is truly a book for all people and highlights the circumstances in a clear and direct manner. The author thoughtfully and in-depth describes the criminal justice system in urban areas and nationally, providing the background, causes, and shortcomings. It clearly describes our current circumstance and how we got here."

—David M. Kochanski, Partner, Shulman Rogers

"*Courts of Law Not Courts of Justice* is a clear, concise primer on our criminal justice system—a system designed to provide individuals with fundamental protection of their freedoms, but which is straining at the seams to do so. Unrelenting dockets, policing practices, self-interested actors, and political pressures combine to undermine trust and render the system unable at times to dispense justice to defendants. Attempts to blame the justice system as a scapegoat for failing to provide 'social justice' often result in frustration boiling over into anger. Much of the misconception of our justice system stems from failure to understand its purposes, its goals, and its limitations. This book is a welcome first step toward a clearer understanding of the justice meted out by our courts."

—Bryan McGahan, Senior Underwriting Counsel, First American Title Insurance Company

"Eric Oberer delivers a captivating introduction to the American justice system. For all who wonder why they don't see justice being served, he answers that question with a timeline of important criminal and constitutional cases that help the reader understand that the law does not always mete out justice. The organization and presentation of landmark Supreme Court cases is perfect for law students and beginning attorneys in the criminal justice world to help them understand the current state of the U.S. criminal justice system with all of its virtues and faults."

—Joe Alfandre, Attorney, Snell & Wilmer, LLP

COURTS OF LAW NOT

COURTS OF JUSTICE

WHY JUSTICE IS HARD TO FIND IN AMERICA

ERIC D. OBERER

atmosphere press

To Wendy Oberer, Zach Oberer,
Darcy Caraballo, and Sonia Maldonado—
truly the salt of the earth.

Preface

As someone who cares deeply about the future of the United States and the ability of its citizens to thrive, I wrote this book to explain things that are simply not taught in classrooms in this country—all the way up through law schools. The theories that are discussed play out in vastly different ways in the real world—in courts of law. Those courts of law are just that, "courts of law," which I would say is contrasted with "courts of justice," as Supreme Court Justice Oliver Wendell Holmes once so eloquently stated. I do not want you to go through years of schooling, particularly about public policy, government, civics, and criminal justice, without knowing these things. There is a very real disconnect between what you may learn in the classroom and the application of those theories in practice. I want you to know what to expect when the rubber meets the road.

I wrote this book to lay out those theories, the history behind those theories, and how those theories interact with real-life interactions of the public with the American justice system. As a former prosecutor in one of the most violent and highest crime cities in America—Baltimore, Maryland—I will explain in detail how we got where we are and why, even though engraved on the highest court of the land, "Equal Justice Under Law" does not always equate to "justice" or "equal" application of that justice. That is not to say that this is a bad thing when put in the perspective of the important aims and goals of the American justice system. But it is an understanding that you, the reader, and the public at-large, should know, understand, accept, and appreciate. If that understanding was made widespread throughout this country, there would be far less discontent—and even civil unrest—over the application of the law in this country—truly in the courts of law rather than the courts of justice.

Table of Contents

The Beginning..3

Part One – Laying the Foundation

Chapter One – In Search of Justice..9
Chapter Two – Interpreting the Constitution 15
Chapter Three – The History, the Rights... 40

Part Two – When the Law Undermines Justice

Chapter Four –Massachusetts v. Lizzie Borden, June 20, 1893 45
Chapter Five – Ohio v. Sam Sheppard, December 21, 1954 53
Chapter Six – California v. O.J. Simpson, October 3, 1995 58
Chapter Seven – Florida v. Casey Anthony, July 5, 2011 63
Chapter Eight – Defining the Boundaries.......................................67

Part Three – Disparities in Justice

Chapter Nine – The Broken Windows Theory 71

Chapter Ten – Civil Unrest: When Citizens Retaliate Against
Unjust Policing Tactics 89

Chapter Eleven – Lack of Resources and Inconsistent
Outcomes 116

Chapter Twelve – Mounting a Defense 126

Part Four – Broken Justice: The Human Element

Chapter Thirteen – When Cops Go Bad 131

Chapter Fourteen – When Attorneys Go Bad 135

Chapter Fifteen – The Jury and Bias 141

Chapter Sixteen – Our Misperceptions 147

Epilogue – A Tale of Two Johnnies 156

Appendix – Honoring the Symbols of Justice 160

Index 165

The Beginning

*"There is no greater tyranny than that which is
perpetrated under the shield of the law and
in the name of justice."* [1]

THERE'S NO BETTER PLACE to start than the beginning: the
birth of a free country. Before the American Revolutionary
War began, King George III's reign of tyranny terrorized the
colonists. There was no individual freedom, and certainly,
there were few protections against being wrongfully accused
of crimes and wrongfully convicted. Rotting away in prison for
crimes one did not commit was commonplace. There was no
fairness. There was no recourse. There was no justice.

The Founding Fathers infused the nascent United States
with principles of individualism, freedom from oppression,
and limited government. They had written lengthy documents
chronicling their fears of tyranny inherent in monarchical and
oligarchic forms of government. James Madison wrote in *The
Federalist Papers,* "[t]he accumulation of all powers, legislative,
executive, and judiciary, in the same hands, whether of one, a
few, or many, and whether hereditary, self-appointed, or elective,

---

[1] Charles-Louis de Secondat, *Baron de la Brède et de Montesquieu,* French
political philosopher and advocate, key proponent of the theory of separation of powers which was implemented in many constitutions throughout
the world, including the United States. From *L'Esprit des lois* (The Spirit
of the Law) (1748).

may justly be pronounced the very definition of tyranny."[2]

Other provocations, such as the Stamp Act of 1765, the Townshend Acts of 1767, the Boston Massacre of 1770, the Boston Tea Party of 1773, the Intolerable Acts of 1774, and Patrick Henry's "give me liberty or give me death" speech of 1775, led to the violent overthrow of the tyrannical King of Great Britain. The Declaration of Independence was signed by the revolutionaries in the North American colonies in 1776, and in that document, Thomas Jefferson listed twenty-seven cases of abuse committed by the British monarchy against the colonies.

It is for those reasons that the Founders envisioned and then implemented significant checks and balances to prevent another horrible, bloody war of insurrection. Among the first fourteen amendments to the United States Constitution (which includes the Bill of Rights), many important protections were addressed and will be discussed in this book. They include:

- *Fourth Amendment*: The right to be free from unreasonable searches and seizures, and requiring that warrants must be based on probable cause.
- *Fifth Amendment*: The right to a grand jury, prohibition of double jeopardy, freedom from compelled self-incrimination, and due process.
- *Sixth Amendment*: The right to assistance of counsel; the right to a trial by an impartial jury; the right to confront witnesses; and the right to a speedy and public trial.
- *Eighth Amendment*: Freedom from excessive bail and cruel and unusual punishment.
- *Fourteenth Amendment*: Freedom from deprivation of life, liberty, and property without due process

---

[2] *The Federalist Papers* No. 47, at 312–13.

of law or equal protection under the law as it pertains to the states.

These amendments, among others, created a framework to guard against the government invading individual freedoms, liberties, and rights. They were aimed at preventing the tyranny that had just been overthrown.

Yet, as you will find throughout this book, these protections have been known to get in the way of finding the truth, of proper recourse, of true justice.

As the author of this book, my intent is to inform, provide insight, and educate the reader on the justice system, the misperceptions about it, and the realities of it. My desire is to provide a new lens through which the American justice system can be viewed...and, hopefully, a more realistic view that comes from years of education, training, and experience as an attorney and former Baltimore prosecutor. Bear in mind that we will delve into politics and some sensitive but important areas. By the end of this book, you will have the historical context, legal theories, and real-world application of these theories to fully grasp why, in the United States, Supreme Court Justice Oliver Wendell Holmes was correct when he said, "this is a court of law, young man, not a court of justice." You will also more fully understand why he said this, building upon the famous quote on the intentions of the Founding Fathers in constructing a legal system—that of Founding Father Benjamin Franklin, who said, "it is better a hundred guilty persons should escape than one innocent person should suffer." Let's start that discussion and change the lens through which we view the American justice system. It's time for a paradigm shift...

PART ONE

LAYING THE FOUNDATION

"[W]hen a strict interpretation of the Constitution, according to the fixed rules which govern the interpretation of laws, is abandoned, and the theoretical opinions of individuals are allowed to control its meaning, we have no longer a Constitution; we are under the government of individual men, who for the time being have power to declare what the Constitution is, according to their own views of what it ought to mean."
—**Benjamin Curtis**, Supreme Court Justice (1851–1857)
Dred Scott v. Sandford, 60 U.S. 393, (1857) (dissenting)

CHAPTER ONE

In Search of Justice

"This is a court of law, young man,
not a court of justice." [3]

I remember many years ago seeing first hand a clear exposition of the difference between law and justice. I was sitting in court and watching a court case unfold where an injured lady was suing a lorry driver for damage and injury caused by his reckless driving.

On the evidence, it was absolutely clear that the lorry driver was at fault although, while he admitted driving the lorry, he persistently denied responsibility for the accident. After a number of independent witnesses had given evidence, it was clear that the injured lady must win.

However, when the case concluded, the judge turned to the lady's barrister with the words, "You presented no evidence that the man was the owner of the lorry. Case dismissed."

The most surprised person in the courtroom that day was the lorry driver.

That was the administration of law, not justice. [4]

---

[3] Justice Oliver Wendell Holmes (1902–1932).

[4] Richard Kennedy, Richard Kennedy & Co. Solicitors: "This is a court of law, young man, not a court of justice" (Apr. 21, 2012), https://richard kennedysolicitors.wordpress.com/2012/04/21/this-is-a-court-of-law-young-man-not-a-court-of-justice/.

YOU MIGHT FIND IT SURPRISING to learn that law and justice in America are not necessarily the same thing. The inimitable Justice Oliver Wendell Holmes, who had become known as "the Great Dissenter" during his twenty-nine years on the U.S. Supreme Court, phrased this problem eloquently, while the second quote, by Solicitor Richard Kennedy, neatly illustrates the conundrum. If perceptions about the American justice system are mistaken, the root of the perceptions lies in the public's expectations about justice itself. Schools, families, and the media teach ideas about justice that are rarely actually to be found in the courtroom.

What Is Justice?

"Equal Justice Under Law" is prominently inscribed on the façade of the United States Supreme Court building in Washington, D.C. According to the Supreme Court's website:

> "[T]he words express the ultimate responsibility of the Supreme Court of the United States. The Court is the highest tribunal in the Nation for all cases and controversies arising under the Constitution or the laws of the United States. As the final arbiter of the law, the Court is charged with ensuring the American people the promise of equal justice under law and, thereby, also functions as guardian and interpreter of the Constitution.[5]

But what is "equal justice?"

According to *Merriam-Webster's Dictionary*, "equal" means comparable or equivalent; roughly the same in quality or amount. "Justice" means the impartial adjustment of conflicting

---

[5] *See* https://www.supremecourt.gov/visiting/visitorsguide-supremecourt.aspx.

claims, the allocation of merited rewards or punishments, the quality of being just, impartial, fair, or morally good, or receiving what one deserves.

It is easy to understand why Americans would expect the United States criminal justice system to produce results that are "just"—that is, results that are merited or deserved as well as morally upright or good. Still, a system of justice that aims to produce just results must compete with the plethora of rights afforded to the accused that is necessary for justice to each individual and holistically, society as a whole, yet not always truly just, merited, or deserved results when taken on a case-by-case basis.

Without historical context, everyday Americans are repeatedly frustrated by a system that does not always produce results that seem just, no matter what inspiring words appear above the courthouse doors in Washington, D.C. or on court buildings across the country.

The United States has always claimed to believe in and stand for the principle of equal justice under law.[6] As American citizens, we expect to benefit from this principle, but the realities of justice administration often do not match our expectations.

If laws are fairly enacted and enforced, justice should follow naturally. There are many reasons why the system does not always achieve this end, however, and those reasons have much to do with the system itself. According to Deborah Rhode, former director of the Center on the Legal Profession at Stanford Law School, "[p]art of the problem is that few individuals are aware of what passes for justice among the have-

---

[6] The phrase "equal justice under law" is derived from Chief Justice Melville Fuller's opinion, in *Caldwell v. Texas*, 137 U.S. 692 (1891), that "the powers of the States in dealing with crime within their borders are not limited, but no State can deprive particular persons or classes of persons of equal and impartial justice under the law."

nots, and many of their perceptions are skewed by idealized portrayals in civics classes, popular media, and right-wing political rhetoric."[7]

The Black Lives Matter movement brought attention to this disparity during one of the worst pandemics in American history. Millions of people saw a video of the senseless killing of an African-American man by police, and people of all races and ethnicities took to the streets around the world to protest and call for justice for George Floyd.

Citizens were in search of fairness. They were in search of recourse. They were in search of justice. But passion and feelings of resentment have sometimes transformed peaceful protests into acts of violence.

What if I told you that the American criminal justice system has never been about justice, that the system itself is not set up to seek out justice, and that it was never designed to find justice? In fact, our system is not equipped to find justice. The United States Constitution, federal laws, and state laws and constitutions intersect, conflict, and sometimes work in tandem to frustrate, not ensure, the justice that people expect.

"A Hundred Guilty Persons..."

The United States' system of law was developed with a great and overriding concern in mind: to protect innocent people charged with crimes they did not commit. Affording justice to the victims of crimes was only a secondary or even tertiary goal. Justice, in and of itself, is not the primary goal of the system that bears the name.

---

[7] Deborah Rhode, "Equal Justice Under Law," presentation from "Ethics at Noon," Markkula Center for Applied Ethics at Santa Clara University, Jan. 1, 2000, https://www.scu.edu/ethics/focus-areas/more/resources/equal-justice-under-law/.

As Benjamin Franklin wrote, "it is better a hundred guilty persons should escape than one innocent person should suffer."[8] As one of the Founding Fathers, Franklin firmly embedded this concept in the nascent country's dialectic. The resulting Constitution requires that criminal defendants be proven guilty beyond a reasonable doubt[9] by a jury of their peers; that trials be provided speedily, with access to effective counsel; that arrestees be *Mirandized*[10] and receive due process; and that the rules of evidence be applied during trial so that evidence obtained in violation of these principles be suppressed. Even the venerable rule of *stare decisis*[11] has been applied to protect the rights of the accused. The very foundation of the American justice system is the desire to avoid sending an innocent person to prison.

Can such a system result in what most of us consider real justice? It simply cannot—neither in theory nor in practice.

The complexities of our criminal justice system can be traced to their beginnings—in revolution against a tyrannical government; through several wars; the Civil Rights Movement; encompassing developing policing practices; changes to and clarifications of the Constitution through caselaw, state, and federal laws and policies; mass protests and society's

---

[8] Letter from Benjamin Franklin to Benjamin Vaughan (Mar. 14, 1785) in *The Works of Benjamin Franklin* Vol. XI (John Bigelow ed., Fed. Ed. 1904).

[9] Reasonable doubt is the "accepted measure of persuasion by which the prosecution must convince the trier of all the essential elements of guilt." C. McCormick, Evidence 321, pp. 681–82 (1954); *See also* 9 J. Wigmore, Evidence, 2497 (3d ed. 1940).

[10] The *Miranda* warnings are familiar to Americans from police procedurals and legal dramas. A person taken into custody must be told of his right to be silent, his right to an attorney, and so on.

[11] *Stare decisis* is a judicial doctrine of respect for precedent. When an appellate court announces a holding, that holding will not be set aside in a later case unless there is good cause for doing so.

changing mores and expectations; lack of federal and state funding; inherent biases and corruption within the system; and imperfect human beings—all of which will be covered in this book in some form or fashion.

These events, and more, have helped shape our criminal justice system into what it is today.

CHAPTER TWO

Interpreting the Constitution

"The liberties of none are safe unless the liberties of all are protected." [12]

WHILE THE FOUNDING FATHERS championed the concepts that would protect those suspected of or charged with crimes, they left it to the Supreme Court to figure out how to do that. Since then, procedural safeguards against unwarranted convictions have played significant roles in criminal jurisprudence, even though this has often forced justice into a back seat.

Marbury v. Madison — Interpreting the Court's Powers

The Supreme Court's power derives from *Marbury v. Madison*, [13] the case in which the Court reserved for itself the final, indubitable right to determine the legality and Constitutionality of virtually every other governmental action. *Marbury*

---

[12] William O. Douglas, *A Living Bill of Rights* (Doubleday, 1961).

[13] *Marbury v. Madison*, 5 U.S. 137 (1803).

established judicial review as one of the most important principles of American law.

The case, like all cases, originated from a disagreement between people. Those people, it so happens, were important people: then-President John Adams and incoming President Thomas Jefferson. Under circumstances that will seem eerily familiar, Adams—on his way out of the White House and bitter at having lost the election of 1800—appointed many of his personal supporters and cronies to positions on the bench and other sorts of "spoils" positions. These appointments were intended to make it more difficult for the incoming administration to develop and implement its own agenda.

And as in many cases, something went wrong. The Senate quickly confirmed Adams' appointments. These appointments, however, were not final until written commissions were delivered to the appointees, and when Jefferson assumed the presidency, some of the commissions remained undelivered. Jefferson instructed his administrators to not deliver them. The stage was therefore set for a monumental showdown of powers.

William Marbury was a businessman in Maryland and a Federalist, a longtime supporter of President Adams, and one of the men who was still waiting for his commission. In late 1801, he asked the Supreme Court to issue a *writ of mandamus*[14] instructing Jefferson's Secretary of State, James Madison, to deliver his commission.

The Court's Chief Justice, John Marshall, authored the opinion. He wrote that Madison was indeed obligated to deliver the commission. If he had stopped there, *Marbury* would be an important case, but perhaps not a foundational one. But he did not stop there.

Chief Justice Marshall carefully examined the law that had

---

[14] A *writ of mandamus* is a court order requiring another court, government entity, organization, or person to perform an act.

been passed by Congress to "give" the Supreme Court jurisdiction over cases like *Marbury.* He found that the statute gave
the Court more powers than it had been granted under the
Constitution, and therefore he ruled that the law was unconstitutional. Congress had tried to give the Court more power
than it had, based on the document that established both of
these branches of the nascent government. By invalidating
that portion of the statute, the Supreme Court assumed for
itself the final word. Going forward, the Court—not Congress,
not the office of the President—would decide whether laws
complied with the Constitution or not. And this was ground-
breaking, even if it meant that poor Marbury did not receive
his promised commission. Because the statute was unconstitutional, the Court refused to issue the requested *writ.*

Powell v. Alabama & *Gideon v. Wainwright* — Interpreting the Sixth Amendment's Right to Counsel

Having assumed this powerful role, the Supreme Court set
about defining the parameters of the criminal justice system
via a number of important decisions. One such case concerned
nine young Black men—the "Scottsboro Boys"—who had been
found guilty of raping two white women. In *Powell v. Alabama,*[15] the Court announced that states must allow criminal
defendants sufficient time to secure lawyers for their trials. It
also held that, in death penalty cases, courts must appoint
counsel to represent defendants if they cannot afford to hire
their own lawyers.

The facts at issue in *Powell* are harrowing. A group of
Black men, aged between thirteen and twenty, were taking a

---

[15] *Powell v. Alabama,* 287 U.S. 45 (1932).

train along with two white women. The women accused the men of raping them. Not surprisingly, given the racism of the times, the men were rapidly tried, convicted, and sentenced to death. They were represented at their trials by poorly prepared lawyers and prevented from contacting their families. The Alabama state supreme court affirmed their convictions. The men appealed, with the assistance of the NAACP, to the Supreme Court.

The opinion that followed was written by Justice George Sutherland:

> *In the light of the ... ignorance and illiteracy of the defendants, their youth, the circumstances of public hostility, the imprisonment and the close surveillance of the defendants by the military forces, the fact that their friends and families were all in other states and communication with them necessarily difficult, and above all that they stood in deadly peril of their lives—we think the failure of the trial court to give them reasonable time and opportunity to secure counsel was a clear denial of due process.*
>
> *But passing that, and assuming their inability, even if opportunity had been given, to employ counsel, ... under the circumstances just stated, the necessity of counsel was so vital and imperative that the failure of the trial court to make an effective appointment of counsel was likewise a denial of due process within the meaning of the Fourteenth Amendment.*

Powell, then, turns upon the Fourteenth Amendment's guarantee of due process and not the Sixth Amendment. Additionally, the Court's stance on the issue was not firm. Only ten years later, in *Betts v. Brady*,[16] the Court significantly limited *Powell*'s reach by holding that a defendant was entitled to

---

[16] *Betts v. Brady*, 316 U.S. 455 (1942).

appointed counsel only if there were special circumstances such as illiteracy or if the defendant was mentally challenged.

With *Gideon v. Wainwright*,[17] however, the Court returned to the principles it had begun sketching out in *Powell*. Ironically, it reached the Court because the defendant, Clarence Gideon, handled his own appeal effectively enough that the Court granted him *certiorari*, meaning that it agreed to hear his case. It appointed respected attorney and future Supreme Court Justice Abe Fortas to argue his case.

Gideon was a small-time crook who had been charged with felony burglary of a pool hall in Florida in 1961. He asked for a court-appointed lawyer, and his request was refused. The state called witnesses who said they had seen him hanging around the pool hall around the time of the break-in, and Gideon was convicted and sentenced to five years in prison.

Fortas could have chosen the safe course for his client and argued that Gideon's request for an attorney should have been granted because he had only an eighth-grade education. But Fortas sensed an opportunity, and he pressed it: he argued that *all* persons charged with felonies were entitled to counsel at trial. This time he focused, and he asked the Court to focus, on the Sixth Amendment.

The Court took him up on the offer. Two months later, the Court ruled that the Fourteenth Amendment's due process clause incorporated the Sixth Amendment's right to counsel. As a result, defendants charged with serious crimes were entitled to court-appointed lawyers, making access to counsel a fundamental Constitutional right. Gideon was retried, and in 1963 he was acquitted.

---

[17] *Gideon v. Wainwright*, 372 U.S. 335 (1963).

Miranda v. Arizona — Interpreting the Fifth Amendment's Self-Incrimination Clause

Gideon ensured that defendants would be represented by attorneys, if they wished, at trial. In another of the Court's monumental opinions, the question was whether criminal suspects could be questioned without being advised of their Constitutional rights. The Court answered, resoundingly, that they could not.

In *Miranda v. Arizona*,[18] the U.S. Supreme Court held that once a suspect was in custody—under arrest and taken back to the police station for questioning, generally—that the suspect's statements could not be used against him at trial unless he first was advised of his right not to incriminate himself. *Miranda* concerns the Fifth Amendment, the privilege in the Constitution to remain silent when questioned by law enforcement. The Fifth Amendment also requires that when a suspect exercises his right and refuses to answer questions put to him by the police, his silence cannot be held against him in court. This is a powerful right that does not exist in many other countries. In England, for example, a suspect is advised that he is not obligated to answer questions but that it may be held against him if he later wants to testify about something in court that he did not tell law enforcement while he was being interrogated. Allowing a suspect to remain silent means that the state must prepare its own case and develop its own evidence without forcing a suspect to cooperate. But the right has little power if suspects don't know about it.

Chief Justice Earl Warren, who led the Court during one of its most activist, expansive phases, authored the opinion. From then on, criminal suspects would have to be told, specifically, that they have the right to remain silent; that anything

---

[18] *Miranda v. Arizona*, 384 U.S. 436 (1966).

they choose to say could be used against them at trial; that they have the right to have an attorney with them; and that an attorney would be appointed to represent them if they could not afford one.

Additionally, once a suspect advised the police officers questioning him that he wanted an attorney, police officers would have to immediately stop questioning him. If the police failed to follow these rules—if they failed to discontinue interrogation once the suspect requested a lawyer or if they failed to advise the suspect of his *Miranda* rights, any incriminating statements that the suspect did say would be suppressed, meaning that they would not be allowed into evidence at trial. This gave the ruling real teeth; cases could be lost, and guilty persons would be released based on violations of these requirements put in place. Suspects could waive their rights and agree to talk to the police without an attorney present, but a waiver would only be effective if it was given "voluntarily, knowingly, and intelligently."

It is always interesting to consider the underlying facts involved in these Supreme Court cases. This case came to the Court following the conviction in Arizona of Ernesto Miranda on charges of kidnapping and rape. Miranda was convicted of his first crime while he was in the eighth grade. He spent time in reform schools and jails and drifted around for several years committing petty crimes. In 1963, an eighteen-year-old woman gave a description of a man who had kidnapped and raped her, and Miranda matched the description and voluntarily accompanied police officers to the station to participate in a lineup. Police suggested that he had been positively identified; shortly afterward, Miranda confessed. However, he had not been advised of all of his rights. After his almost inevitable conviction, he represented himself in filing an appeal, and when his case was accepted by the Supreme Court, lawyers were appointed to argue for him. They won.

The case was retried, this time without the evidence of Miranda's confession. He was again convicted and sentenced to twenty to thirty years imprisonment but was paroled after serving a few years. A few years later, he was killed in a fight in a bar. This was an ignominious end for a man whose name would become virtually synonymous with the Fifth Amendment.

Critics of *Miranda*, then, did not have to look far for reasons to disapprove. Men like Ernesto Miranda would benefit from the ruling. Victims of crime would, in general, not.

Mapp v. Ohio — Interpreting the Fourth Amendment's Searches and Seizures Clause

The right of the people to be secure in their persons, houses, papers, and effects, against unreasonable searches and seizures, shall not be violated, and no Warrants shall issue, but upon probable cause, supported by Oath or affirmation, and particularly describing the place to be searched, and the persons or things to be seized.

Mapp v. Ohio[19] is an important Fourth Amendment case. It stands for the proposition that when the government obtains evidence as a result of an unconstitutional search, the evidence cannot be used at trial to prove the defendant's guilt. You might think of *Mapp* as providing a penalty for ignoring the Constitution's prohibition on warrantless searches and seizures.

Cleveland police officers searched Dollree Mapp's home in 1957, hoping to find a bombing suspect. They had not sought a warrant first. Although they did not locate the suspect in Mapp's home, they did find a collection of illegal pornography.

---

[19] *Mapp v. Ohio*, 367 U.S. 643 (1961).

Mapp was convicted of violating Ohio law against possessing lewd and lascivious material.

Ohio's highest court decided that the search had, in fact, been unlawful without a warrant, but they refused to do anything about it. Federal courts were required to exclude evidence obtained in violation of the Fourth Amendment, but a 1949 case, *Wolf v. Colorado*,[20] had excepted state courts from that requirement. The Supreme Court granted *certiorari* and then reversed.

Without some consequence to be applied, Justice Tom Clark wrote, the Fourth Amendment would be nothing but empty words and "might as well be stricken from the Constitution." And, "[t]o hold otherwise is to grant the right but, in reality, to withhold its privilege and enjoyment[.]"

Of course, applying the exclusionary rule in cases like *Mapp* means that criminals may go free. We might not be too concerned about that if the criminal is someone like Dollree Mapp, a man who was, for the most part, minding his own business when the police barged in, seized evidence, and then charged him with a non-violent crime. Applying the rule in more serious cases, however, means that murderers, rapists, arsonists, and others will also sometimes avoid being held responsible for their crimes. However, the Court emphasized the importance of applying the law without making exceptions.

Katz v. United States — Interpreting the Fourth Amendment's Privacy Clause

Often when the Supreme Court has provided protections for people charged with crimes, it has acted by ruling that evidence obtained in impermissible ways cannot be used at trial.

---

[20] *Wolf v. Colorado*, 338 U.S. 25 (1949).

Miranda had to do with a criminal suspect's own statements; statements are one kind of evidence that can be used to convict. Another kind of evidence is what lawyers call *real* evidence: a gun used in a shooting; a baggie of marijuana; the shoe that matches a print left in the dirt beneath the window of a burglarized home. The Fourth Amendment prohibits warrantless searches and seizures. Over time, the Court has developed guidelines for what a "search" or "seizure" is and for when evidence like this found without a warrant may be used at a suspect's trial.

The Founders probably intended for the Fourth Amendment to apply primarily to a person's own body or home, as these were traditionally considered "private." In *Katz v. United States*,[21] the Supreme Court extended the Fourth Amendment's protection to other areas beyond the "persons, houses, papers, and effects" specified in the Constitution to any areas an individual "seeks to preserve as private, even in an area accessible to the public."

Who were the players involved, and what happened to bring this case to the Court? Charles Katz lived in Los Angeles, CA, and had long been involved in sports betting. He was a prolific gambler, specializing in college basketball by the 1960s, and he placed his bets using a telephone booth near his apartment. The FBI, however, was listening in on his phone calls, and once a sufficient number of recordings had been assembled, they arrested Katz and charged him with a federal crime. The recordings had been obtained through a listening device placed in the telephone booth, but no one had first obtained a warrant.

Katz's lawyer moved to suppress the recordings, arguing that they were the result of a warrantless search in violation of the Fourth Amendment. The trial judge declined the

---

[21] *Katz v. United States*, 389 U.S. 347 (1967).

request, and Katz was convicted. On appeal, a three-judge panel upheld the conviction, ruling that no warrant was required because the listening device was not inside the telephone booth wall and was, therefore, not a search. In 1967, the Supreme Court reversed.

In doing so, the Court set aside the search and seizure analysis that had, until then, required courts to decide whether a trespass onto private property was involved and whether law enforcement had "penetrated" a protected area (by drilling holes to install a listening device, for example). That analysis was based on *Olmstead v. United States*,[22] a wiretap case. Instead, the Court held that courts should apply a more flexible, functional test to consider whether a person would reasonably expect privacy in using a particular space, even if that space was not a personal residence or privately owned.

Justice Potter Stewart wrote:

> *The petitioner [Katz] has strenuously argued that the booth was a 'constitutionally protected area.' The government has maintained with equal vigor that it was not. But this effort to decide whether a given 'area,' viewed in the abstract, is 'constitutionally protected' deflects attention from the problem presented by this case. For the Fourth Amendment protects people, not places. What a person knowingly exposes to the public, even in his own home or office, is not a subject of Fourth Amendment protection. But what he seeks to preserve as private, even in an area accessible to the public, may be constitutionally protected.*[23]

---

[22] *Olmstead v. United States*, 277 U.S. 428 (1928).

[23] *Katz*, 389 U.S. at 352.

The Court continued:

We conclude that the underpinnings of Olmstead [and similar cases] have been so eroded by our subsequent decisions that the "trespass" doctrine there enunciated can no longer be regarded as controlling. The Government's activities in electronically listening to and recording the petitioner's words violated the privacy on which he justifiably relied while using the telephone booth and thus constituted a 'search and seizure' within the meaning of the Fourth Amendment.[24]

Generally, a person using a phone booth expects that his or her phone call will be private, even if the booth itself is in a public place. Therefore, the Court held the government violated the Fourth Amendment by listening in on Katz's phone calls without first obtaining a warrant. The evidence of Katz's bets should have been suppressed at his trial.

Terry v. Ohio and *Illinois v. Wardlow* — Interpreting the Fourth Amendment's Stop-and-Frisk Clause

The Fourth, Fifth, and Sixth Amendments generally assume an arrest or prosecution. In the centuries since the Constitution was drafted, however, law enforcement agencies have evolved methods for obtaining information about crimes outside those contexts in order to establish probable cause. One such method is what we now call the *Terry* stop. In *Terry v. Ohio*,[25] the U.S. Supreme Court held that such stops—in which an officer stops a person for questioning and pats them down

---

[24] *Id.* at 353.

[25] *Terry v. Ohio*, 392 U.S. 1 (1968).

for weapons or drugs—are permissible under certain circumstances.

On a late October afternoon in 1963, Martin McFadden, a detective with the Cleveland police department, became suspicious of the activities of two men, John Terry and Richard Chilton. McFadden believed the men were planning a robbery. It turns out that his suspicions were correct. When he patted them down, McFadden found two concealed pistols, and the men were arrested and charged. Terry and Chilton appealed, arguing that the weapons were the product of an illegal search.

By the time the case reached the Supreme Court, only Terry's conviction was at issue. Chief Justice Earl Warren authored the opinion. In *Terry*, the Court ruled that police officers may conduct a limited pat-down for weapons to ensure the officers' safety, so long as the suspects were observed behaving suspiciously beforehand. These pat-downs are searches and, therefore, subject to the Fourth Amendment. Nevertheless, the Court held under the right circumstances, they are constitutionally permissible. Ultimately, the inquiry turns on whether the officer's actions are reasonable in light of the facts and circumstances surrounding the search. In this case, given the risk to the officer's life, it was reasonable to perform a limited pat-down, and the inconvenience to the individual was relatively small.

In reaching this conclusion, the Court recognized that stop and frisks would potentially harm the communities in which they were performed. Law enforcement is less effective when the relationship between the community and the police is strained. Community members are less likely to approach police officers voluntarily if they fear being patted down. In permitting *Terry* stops, the Court balanced these competing interests and came down on the side of law enforcement.

The Court built upon this standard in *Illinois v. Wardlow*,[26] permitting officers with reasonable, articulable suspicion of criminal activity to conduct a brief stop. That might not sound very different from *Terry*, but the devil, as they say, is in the details. In *Wardlow*, two uniformed officers cruised into an area known for drug activity. The defendant, a Black man, spotted the officers and ran away; they chased him, patted him down, and found a handgun on his person. He was tried and convicted of possessing the weapon. The key point here is that the officers had not observed Wardlow doing anything suspicious before they chased him. The question was whether his attempt to run away was, in and of itself, enough to justify the officers' suspicions.

Illinois' highest court held that it was not. The state requested *certiorari*, and the Supreme Court agreed to hear the case. They reversed, siding with the prosecution. Justice William Rehnquist held that a person's nervous behavior was a basis for performing a *Terry* stop consistent with Fourth Amendment principles. Attempting to run away was an obvious form of evasion, according to Justice Rehnquist. Taking the man's attempt to run with the fact that he was in an area known for the narcotics trade, it was reasonable for the police to stop him to investigate further. Since they could stop him, they could also pat him down; as a result, the handgun they found on him was not a product of an illegal search.

Missing, perhaps, from the Court's consideration of relevant factors was whether there might be other reasons for Black men to run away from law enforcement officers. The opinion focused on the goals of so-called community policing, including reducing crime. It did not focus on whether permitting stops and pat-downs in situations like those before the Court would worsen relations between the community and the police, which is unfortunate.

---

[26] *Illinois v. Wardlow*, 528 U.S. 119 (2000).

Klopfer v. North Carolina — Interpreting the Sixth Amendment's Right to a Speedy and Public Trial by an Impartial Jury

The right to a jury trial is one of the most fundamental rights inherent in the American justice system. As Alexander Hamilton put it in *The Federalist*, No. 83:

> *The strongest argument in its favor is, that it is a security against corruption. As there is always more time and better opportunity to tamper with a standing body of magistrates than with a jury summoned for the occasion, there is room to suppose that a corrupt influence would more easily find its way to the former than to the latter. The force of this consideration is, however, diminished by others. The sheriff, who is the summoner of ordinary juries, and the clerks of courts, who have the nomination of special juries, are themselves standing officers, and, acting individually, may be supposed more accessible to the touch of corruption than the judges, who are a collective body. It is not difficult to see, that it would be in the power of those officers to select jurors who would serve the purpose of the party as well as a corrupted bench.*
>
> *In the next place, it may fairly be supposed, that there would be less difficulty in gaining some of the jurors promiscuously taken from the public mass, than in gaining men who had been chosen by the government for their probity and good character. But making every deduction for these considerations, the trial by jury must still be a valuable check upon corruption. It greatly multiplies the impediments to its success.*
>
> *As matters now stand, it would be necessary to corrupt both court and jury; for where the jury have gone evidently wrong, the court will generally grant a new trial, and it would be in most cases of little use to practice*

upon the jury, unless the court could be likewise gained. Here then is a double security; and it will readily be perceived that this complicated agency tends to preserve the purity of both institutions. By increasing the obstacles to success, it discourages attempts to seduce the integrity of either.

The temptations to prostitution which the judges might have to surmount, must certainly be much fewer, while the co-operation of a jury is necessary, than they might be, if they had themselves the exclusive determination of all causes.

A jury drawn from the defendant's community will necessarily be made up of random citizens. These citizens serve on a single jury and then go about their lives. They arrive for trial free of most of the sorts of preconceptions and prejudices that judges or government officials can develop over many years of hearing cases. This is the power and the enormous value represented by the Constitution's guarantee of the right to trial by jury. The Founders knew that power concentrated in a single person led to tyranny, and that was why they so carefully checked and balanced the powers of the three branches of government. They did much the same by ensuring that twelve people, and not one, would decide the fates of Americans charged with criminal offenses.

A criminal defendant is not only entitled to a jury trial; he or she is entitled to a speedy one, thanks to the Sixth Amendment. Like the other first ten amendments, the Sixth Amendment initially applied only to the federal government. In *Klopfer v. North Carolina,*[27] the Supreme Court extended that guarantee to the states.

Like many cases arising during the turbulent nineteen-sixties, the case arose from an act of civil disobedience. Peter

---

[27] *Klopfer v. North Carolina*, 386 U.S. 213 (1967).

Klopfer was an activist and a professor at Duke University in North Carolina, where Jim Crow was still the law of the land. He was indicted by a grand jury for criminal trespass and then pled not guilty. His jury hung, meaning they could not reach a verdict. The state employed an unusual maneuver that allowed them to dismiss the case but recharge Professor Klopfer in the future.

The professor's attorney appealed the court's grant of the prosecutor's motion. He argued that it violated the right to a speedy trial as it would allow the case to linger on, possibly interfering with the defendant's right to travel to other states and his professional activities. North Carolina's highest court affirmed the trial court, finding that the dismissal was the exercise of a kind of prosecutorial discretion. A defendant should not be allowed to pressure the state to seek a trial before it is ready to proceed, according to the court.

The Supreme Court took the case partly in order to establish that the Sixth Amendment right to a speedy trial applied to the states through the Fourteenth Amendment, and it did that. In addition, the Court, via Chief Justice Earl Warren, took issue with North Carolina's exercise of "prosecutorial discretion." There was no precedent for what Justice Warren called an "extraordinary legal procedure."

In fact, the Court relayed a detailed history of the development of the right. It developed as far back as 1166, in the English Assize Court and with the Magna Carta in 1215. The drafters of the Constitution were very familiar with these traditions, had studied English common law, and wanted such principles to apply in the new country. Clearly, it extended to the federal government as the Constitution specified. At the time of the Court's opinion in *Klopfer,* it was also provided for in one form or another in each of the states. Therefore, it was "one of the most basic rights preserved by our Constitution."

The Court looked to its decision in *Gideon,* also decided

under the Sixth Amendment. It would be inconsistent to extend one of the Sixth Amendment's guarantees to the states and not another. The Court's decision in *Klopfer* meant from that point on, all defendants charged with crimes could demand a speedy trial.

In subsequent decisions, the Court dealt with other significant jury-related rights. In *Apodaca v. Oregon*,[28] the Court declined to require that state court defendants be convicted by the vote of a unanimous twelve-person jury. Most of the states required this anyway. In 2020, the Court revisited the issue and changed its mind. In *Ramos v. Louisiana*,[29] a man was convicted of murder by a vote of ten to two, meaning that ten jurors found him guilty and two did not. He appealed and argued that Louisiana's law allowing non-unanimous convictions was a vestige of the state's Jim Crow system. The Supreme Court agreed with him and reversed his conviction, finding that the Sixth Amendment's requirement of a unanimous verdict, in fact, applies equally to the states.

Mattox v. United States — Interpreting the Sixth Amendment's Witness Confrontation Clause

Not all of the cases we must consider took place during the civil rights era. In *Mattox v. United States*,[30] decided in the late nineteenth century, the Supreme Court enshrined one of the most important principles of criminal trial practice: the right of the defendant to confront the witnesses against him.

Clyde Mattox allegedly murdered a man and was convicted following a trial in which hearsay evidence was offered against

---

[28] *Apodaca v. Oregon*, 406 U.S. 404 (1972).

[29] *Ramos v. Louisiana*, 140 S. Ct. 1390, 206 L.Ed.2d 583 (2020).

[30] *Mattox v. United States*, 156 U.S. 237 (1895).

him. Under the rules of evidence, hearsay is any statement made outside of court and offered to prove the truth of the statement itself. A witness who testifies, "A man told me that John Brown is a bad man," is offering hearsay if the point of the evidence is to prove that John Brown is a bad man. There was a good reason for allowing hearsay to come in at Mattox's trial; a witness had died, and the court allowed the jury to hear things that the witness had previously said under oath. But that, of course, meant that Mattox could not cross-examine the witness about the statements at his trial.

The U.S. Supreme Court took the appeal, and ultimately Mattox lost. He lost because he had been given the opportunity to confront the witness during a previous trial, so he hadn't really been deprived of his right to cross-examine. But in reaching the decision, the Court thoroughly discussed the purpose of the Sixth Amendment's Confrontation Clause. The Court explained that:

> *The primary object of the Confrontation Clause is to prevent depositions or ex parte affidavits from being used against the defendant in lieu of a personal examination and cross-examination of the witness in which the accused has an opportunity to compel him to stand face to face with the jury so that [the defendant] may look at him and judge, by his demeanor upon the stand and the manner in which he gives his testimony, whether he is worthy of belief.*

The Court agreed that, while the Confrontation Clause of the Sixth Amendment is a fundamental constitutional right, Mattox pushed the bounds of the clause past its plausible limit. In this case, the court concluded:

> *To say that a criminal, after having once been convicted by the testimony of a certain witness, should go scot [sic]*

free simply because death has closed the mouth of that witness, would be carrying his constitutional protection to an unwarrantable extent.

Courts have since had many, many opportunities to refine the law concerning this issue.

United States v. Salerno — Interpreting the Eighth Amendment's Excessive Bail Clause

The Eighth Amendment provides: "Excessive bail shall not be required, nor excessive fines imposed, nor cruel and unusual punishments inflicted." Punishments for crimes must be proportional to the offense, and the conditions imposed on defendants who request release pending trial must not be unreasonable considering the crimes charged.

So, for example, federal courts are allowed to detain a person through trial if the person is potentially dangerous to the community.[31] This is so even though bail has often been understood as intended to ensure that defendants on trial remain in the state and don't abscond. The Supreme Court emphasized that bail's purpose is not so limited.

[W]e reject the proposition that the Eighth Amendment categorically prohibits the government from pursuing other admittedly compelling interests through regulation of pretrial release.[32] ... The only arguable substantive limitation of the Bail Clause is that the government's proposed conditions of release or detention not be "excessive" in light of the perceived evil. Detention prior to trial of

---

[31] *United States v. Salerno*, 481 U.S. 739 (1987).

[32] *Id.* at 753.

arrestees charged with serious felonies who are found af-
ter an adversary hearing to pose a threat to the safety of
individuals or to the community which no condition of
release can dispel satisfies this requirement.

In light of this test, what is "excessive" bail? The sum required should be set at a point that is reasonably calculated to
ensure the governmental interest—whether that is protecting
the public or minimizing the risk of flight—and no higher.

Furman v. Georgia — Interpreting the Eighth Amendment's Cruel and Unusual Punishment Clause

In addition to bail, the Eighth Amendment also prohibits
"cruel and unusual punishment," a term whose meaning has
been considered by a number of important opinions. One such
case was *Furman v. Georgia.*[33]

It is worth pointing out that although we often discuss the
facts at issue in cases as if they were clear and settled and un-
disputed, in reality, they often are not. By the time a particular
case is on appeal, a trial has been held, the facts have been
litigated, and whichever version of the facts has been chosen
by a jury is the version considered by the appellate court. In
Furman, everyone agreed that the defendant, William Furman, slipped into a home one night in Georgia and startled the
resident. What happened next was disputed. Furman claimed
at trial that he tried to escape but stumbled, his gun went off,
and he accidentally killed the home's owner. But the prosecution claimed, and Furman had told police previously, that he
intentionally fired his weapon.

The state side-stepped the issue and charged Furman with
felony murder, meaning that he had killed someone while he

---

[33] *Furman v. Georgia*, 408 U.S. 238 (1972).

was committing another felony, burglary. As a result, his intent to kill didn't really matter so long as he intended to commit the burglary. A jury found him guilty, and he was sentenced to die for the crime.

The appeal reached the Supreme Court, and it reversed, holding that imposing the death penalty based on the facts of the case was cruel and unusual punishment, and thus prohibited by the Eighth Amendment. So Furman won. Unfortunately, the individual justices could not agree on a rationale for the decision. Several justices wrote their own opinions explaining why they believed the punishment was unduly harsh, but their reasons for believing this were different.

One of them, Justice William Brennan, wrote an opinion that described four factors worthy of consideration in the Eighth Amendment context. They are: whether the punishment is so severe that it is "degrading to human dignity," especially in the case of torture; whether the punishment is inflicted in a completely arbitrary way; whether the punishment has been firmly rejected by society; and whether a severe punishment is "patently unnecessary."

When the Court released the *Furman* opinion, all death sentences then in effect in the country were converted to sentences of life imprisonment. The states and Congress were required to review their death penalty legislation to ensure that it would be administered in a way that would not be considered cruel and unusual going forward.

During the four years that followed, many states enacted new statutes for imposing the death penalty. Some of the new provisions required bifurcating trials, meaning that the defendant would be tried to determine his guilt first and afterward separately tried to determine whether to sentence him to death. Additionally, standards were provided to ensure that judges and juries considering the death penalty would not act arbitrarily or capriciously.[34]

Thus far, we have considered a number of Constitutional rights held by people who are suspected of or charged with criminal conduct. The tables on the following pages provide a convenient summary of the relevant cases.

The Fourth Amendment	
Protection from unreasonable searches and seizures	Reasonable expectation of privacy
Weeks v. United States, 232 U.S. 383 (1914)	*Katz v. United States*, 389 U.S. 347 (1967)
Mapp v. Ohio, 367 U.S. 643 (1961)	
Terry v. Ohio, 392 U.S. 1 (1968)	
Illinois v. Wardlow, 528 U.S. 119 (2000)	

The Fifth Amendment
Protection against self-incrimination
Miranda v. Arizona, 384 U.S. 436 (1966)

---

[34] *Gregg v. Georgia, Proffitt v. Florida, Jurek v. Texas, Woodson v. North Carolina,* and *Roberts v. Louisiana*, 428 U.S. 153 (1976).

The Sixth Amendment		
Representation by counsel	Speedy and public trial by an impartial jury	Confrontation of witnesses
Gideon v. Wainwright, 372 U.S. 335 (1963)	*Klopfer v. North Carolina*, 386 U.S. 213 (1967)	*Mattox v. United* States, 156 U.S. 237 (1895)
Powell v. Alabama, 287 U.S. 45 (1932)		

The Eighth Amendment	
Reasonable Bail	Prohibition against Cruel and Unusual Punishment
Stack v. Boyle, 342 U.S. 1 (1951)	*Furman v. Georgia*, 408 U.S. 238 (1972)
United States v. Salerno, 481 U.S. 739 (1987)	*Gregg v. Georgia*, 428 U.S. 153 (1976)
	Proffitt v. Florida, 428 U.S. 242 (1976)
	Jurek v. Texas, 428 U.S. 262 (1976)
	Woodson v. North Carolina, 428 U.S. 280 (1976)
	Roberts v. Louisiana, 428 U.S. 325 (1976)

The Fifth & Fourteenth Amendments	
Substantive and procedural due process	
Mapp v. Ohio, 367 U.S. 643 (1961)	*Klopfer v. North Carolina*, 386 U.S. 213 (1967)
Gideon v. Wainwright, 372 U.S. 335 (1963)	*Powell v. Alabama*, 287 U.S. 45 (1932)

CHAPTER THREE

The History, the Rights...

"When we lose the right to be different,
we lose the privilege to be free." [35]

TO RECAP, THE STORY underlying much of the United States' jurisprudence is the story of a rebellion against a tyrannical government. The colonists chafed beneath the various oppressions committed against them by the British monarchy, and they established a new kind of country, one that would prioritize the individual rights of its citizens at the expense of government...even if that means guilty people sometimes go free when these rights are violated by law enforcement. We established an interconnected system of rights to protect people accused of committing crimes from being railroaded by the government, and in *Marbury*, we ensured that the Supreme Court would be the ultimate arbiter, responsible for interpreting and enforcing those rights:

---

[35] Justice Charles Evan Hughes, Address at Faneuil Hall, Boston, Massachusetts, on the 150th anniversary of the Battle of Bunker Hill (June 17, 1925).

- *Mapp* required that evidence obtained via illegal search or seizure is inadmissible at trial (the "Exclusionary Rule"). The Court also held that protections against the federal government contained in the Fourth Amendment apply to state governments via the Fourteenth Amendment's due process clause. The Court in *Gideon* and *Klopfer* similarly applied the Sixth Amendment rights to counsel and speedy trial to the states, and *Miranda* applied the Fifth Amendment to the states.
- *Gideon* required that legal counsel must be provided to anyone charged with a felony.
- *Miranda* required that a person cannot be compelled to incriminate himself and that the police must advise arrestees of their constitutional rights before they are questioned.
- *Katz* further defined what could be searched and seized without a warrant and described a right of a reasonable expectation of privacy in one's person and surroundings.
- *Terry* and *Wardlow* defined how far police could go in performing stop-and-frisks while patrolling in the community.
- *Klopfer* guaranteed the right to a speedy and public trial by an impartial jury.
- *Mattox* solidified the right to confront witnesses against the accused.
- *Salerno* and other decisions protected citizens against the imposition of excessive bail.
- *Furman* made clear that states may not impose cruel and unusual punishments.

We are taught that the United States criminal justice system is designed to deliver fairness and equality when remedying wrongs, but in reality, the system is designed to protect the rights of the accused and to ensure that innocent people are not convicted of crimes. We are taught these principles in the abstract, based upon what the Constitution says and what the Supreme Court says, but most of us will never be in a position to argue a case—or, even more unlikely, decide one—at the Supreme Court. Most of us will interact with the law in state and municipal courtrooms, where trial judges and juries receive evidence, listen to witnesses, decide the facts, and then apply the law. What really transpires in the courtroom in real cases involving real people isn't always fair or equal, as the cases in the next section will show.

These are but a handful of famous criminal cases. They are worth reviewing because they demonstrate what happens when the rights of criminal defendants interfere with providing justice. These cases hinge upon the rights we have just reviewed, arising from the Fourth, Fifth, Sixth, and Fourteenth Amendments. But they also hinge upon the specific standard of proof required for conviction in a criminal case—the high burden of proof known as "beyond a reasonable doubt."

The term "beyond a reasonable doubt" does not appear in the Constitution. In fact, the Supreme Court has expressed the view that the reasonable doubt standard only "crystalliz[ed] ... as late as 1798."[36] Nevertheless, it is the standard used throughout the country. The job of a judge or jury is not to determine the truth in any given case. Instead, unless the accused pleads guilty, "the prosecution must convince the trier of all the essential elements of guilt" beyond a reasonable doubt.[37]

---

[36] *In re Winship*, 397 U.S. 358 (1970).

[37] C. McCormick, EVIDENCE § 321, pp. 681–82 (1954); *See also* 9 J. Wigmore, EVIDENCE, 2497 (3d ed. 1940).

PART TWO

WHEN THE LAW UNDERMINES JUSTICE

"Defense counsel need present nothing, even if he knows what the truth is. ... If he can confuse a witness, even a truthful one, or make him appear at a disadvantage, unsure or indecisive, that will be his normal course. Our interest in not convicting the innocent permits counsel to put the State to its proof, to put the State's case in the worse possible light, regardless of what he thinks or knows to be the truth."
—**Byron White**, Supreme Court Justice (1962-1993)
United States v. Wade, 388 U.S. 218 (1967)

CHAPTER FOUR

Massachusetts v. Lizzie Borden, June 20, 1893

Fifth Amendment Right Against Self-Incrimination [38]

THE BORDENS WERE a prosperous family. Andrew Borden had worked hard, first building a business that manufactured and sold home furnishings and—somewhat disconcertingly—caskets, and then as a real estate developer in Fall River, Massachusetts. He was a respected man in the town and was a board member of two banks. But he was very likely a difficult man to live with. Despite his affluence, Andrew Borden lived with his second wife, Abby, and his daughters, Lizzie and Emma, in a home with no indoor plumbing, even though most people of similar stature had installed this convenience some time before. Lizzie and Abby were not close. She called her stepmother "Mrs. Borden." There were apparently other sources of long-simmering tensions. On one occasion, Andrew Borden killed a flock of pigeons that Lizzie had been keeping as pets. Andrew had also been making generous gifts to Abby's family, and this must have rankled his daughters. The crime

---

[38] Douglas Linder, "The Trial of Lizzie Borden: An Account," famous-trials.com, https://famous-trials.com/lizzieborden/1437-home.

that would occur within their home would be remembered for many years to come.

On the evening of August 3, 1892, the family had a guest, John Morse, Lizzie's uncle and the brother of Andrew's first wife. He was given the use of a guest room. He may have been visiting to discuss business with Andrew. In any event, the entire family had been ill for days before John arrived. They may have eaten spoiled mutton, or, as Abby apparently suspected, they might have been poisoned. Andrew Borden was a successful man but not a popular one.

Andrew, Abby, Lizzie, John, and the Bordens' maid, Bridget "Maggie" Sullivan, were all at breakfast on the morning of August 4. Afterward, Andrew and John retired to the sitting room for their talk. After about an hour, John departed to attend to business in town and to visit a niece who lived nearby. He intended to return for lunch at about noon. Andrew took his regular morning walk at 9:00 a.m.

It was Lizzie's task to tend to the guest room, but for some reason, that morning, Abby went upstairs to make the bed. Whoever attacked her faced her directly. Abby knew who her killer was and must have known that she was going to die. The killer struck Abby on the side of the head with a hatchet. The violence of the initial blow spun Abby around, and she fell face down onto the floor. Seventeen more blows of the axe fell to the back of Abby's head.

Andrew returned home at about 10:30 a.m. For some reason, his key would not open the door. He summoned Maggie, and she was also unable to open the door. Maggie would later testify in court that she heard Lizzie laughing from the top of the stairs as Andrew struggled to get inside.

According to Lizzie, once her father had gained entry to the house, she helped him to remove his boots and brought him his slippers so that he could lie down on the sofa for a nap. Then she suggested that Maggie visit a local department store that was advertising a sale that day. Maggie, however, did not feel well. She went to her own bedroom on the third floor of the house to rest instead.

Just after eleven, Maggie heard Lizzie calling her from downstairs: "Maggie! Come quick! Father's dead; somebody came in and killed him!" Maggie was horrified to discover that Andrew was lying on the couch, having been struck many times with a hatchet. One of his eyes was neatly split in two, suggesting that he had been asleep when the killer struck. His wounds were fresh. The family's neighbor, Dr. Bowen, was brought to the house. He made the obvious determination that Andrew was dead. The task was now one for the police.

Detectives began by questioning the other occupants of the house, including Lizzie. Her responses were, by turns, odd or self-contradictory. At first, she told the detectives that she was not home at the time of the attacks and that as she was returning home, she had heard noises—the sound of someone groaning, calling for help, or scraping. Not long after, she told them that she had heard nothing and walked into the house, having no idea that anything was amiss. She said that as far as she knew, her stepmother Abby had gone to visit a sick friend, but she thought she had returned. Abby had not, however, appeared to see what the police were doing in the house, so it was suggested that someone go and look for her. Maggie and a neighbor, Mrs. Churchill, climbed the stairs about halfway and immediately saw Abby's body lying on the floor.

Lizzie's behavior at this point was suspicious. Police officers said that she seemed calm and composed. She was giving confusing and contradictory statements. No one, however, checked to see if there were any bloodstains on her body underneath her clothing. A search of her room was made, but it was cursory and quick. Later on, explaining their lackadaisical investigation at trial, the policemen claimed that Lizzie had not been feeling well.

A search of the rest of the house yielded several hatchets and axes in the basement, as well as a hatchet head with a broken handle. It was this last item that was probably the murder weapon, as the break in the wood seemed to be recent, and it looked like someone had tried to cover the head with ashes to make it appear as though it had not been used for some time.

Investigators soon learned that Lizzie had recently purchased a weakened form of cyanide (prussic acid) at a local pharmacy. They arranged for testing of the victims' stomach contents during their autopsies, but no evidence of the poison was found. Lizzie claimed that she wanted the acid to clean her furs, although prussic acid is not generally used for this purpose.

For some reason, the police also failed to secure the house and permitted Lizzie, her friend Alice Russell, and John to spend the night of the murders there. Rumors later flew that John had slept in the room where Abby had been killed, but he claimed that he slept in the attic. Officers were stationed around the house. One of them claimed that Lizzie and Alice entered the cellar carrying a kerosene lamp and a bucket. Both women came out, and then Lizzie went back in. He said that he could not see what Lizzie was doing in the cellar but that she was bent over a sink.

By the next morning, the house was surrounded by people who had heard about the crimes and who were clamoring for a peek inside. The police delayed yet another day and then finally conducted a more thorough search of the house. This time they looked at Lizzie and Emma's clothing and seized the broken hatchet head. On the night of August 6, Lizzie was advised that she was a suspect in her father and stepmother's murders. On the morning of August 7, Alice walked into the kitchen to discover Lizzie destroying a dress. Lizzie said that the dress was covered in paint. No one knows whether it was the dress that Lizzie was wearing three days before.

An inquest was held the next day. Lizzie was required to appear but she was not permitted to have her family attorney with her while she answered questions. She might have been taking morphine as well; it had been prescribed for her to calm her nerves. As a result, her testimony may not be particularly trustworthy. Still, her demeanor remained strange. She refused to answer many of the questions asked of her, even when the questions would have helped her.

She continued to give conflicting accounts of her activities and whereabouts on the day of the murders. At one point, she said that she was in the kitchen reading when her father came home. Later she said she was in the dining room ironing clothes. Then she said that she was coming down the stairs (which, if true, possibly corroborates Maggie's recollection that she heard Lizzie laughing from the stairs). Lizzie stuck to her claim that she had helped her father take off his boots and put on his slippers even though crime scene photographs showed that Andrew was wearing his boots when he was killed.

Things did not look good for Lizzie. Unsurprisingly, she was arrested on August 11 and taken to the town jail. Her trial got underway in June of 1893. However, Lizzie and her defense attorneys would not have to explain her strange testimony at the inquest during her criminal trial. The court concluded that because she had been forced to testify without the benefit of her attorney's presence and counsel, her testimony was involuntary and therefore violated her Fifth Amendment privilege against compelled self-incrimination. She should have been warned before her appearance that she had the right to remain silent.

Lawyers for the prosecution and the defense focused on the hatchet head that had been found in the Borden family basement. The evidence concerning whether it had been the murder weapon was by no means overwhelming. One of the police officers testified that he saw a hatchet handle lying near the head, but another officer said there had not been such a handle in the basement. The state argued that the murderer must have removed the handle because it was covered in the victims' blood. Alice told the jury about Lizzie's attempt to burn her dress several days after the crime. Lizzie's lawyers offered no evidence to contradict Alice's testimony on this issue.

Witnesses gave varying testimony about whether Lizzie was in the house when Andrew and Abby were murdered. Maggie, the maid, said that Lizzie and her father were together in a downstairs room when she climbed the stairs to her bedroom. Lizzie claimed that she left the house and went out to the barn for twenty to thirty minutes. She called two men who confirmed her story, saying that they saw Lizzie leaving the barn at around 11:03 a.m. Maggie testified that Lizzie called her to report her father's murder at 11:10 a.m. but would not let her come into the room and told her to run for the doctor. The doctor estimated that Andrew had died at about 11:00 a.m.

No one was permitted to testify about Lizzie's purchase of prussic acid in the days before the crime. The judge ruled that the evidence was not relevant enough to overcome the risk that it would prejudice the jury against the defendant.

In his closing argument, Lizzie's defense attorney, A.V. Jennings, told the jurors that "there is not one particle of direct evidence in this case from beginning to end against Lizzie A. Borden. There is not a spot of blood, there is not a weapon that they have connected with her in any way, shape or fashion." The jury deliberated for about an hour and a half and returned an acquittal.

We might find this result extremely difficult to believe today. How could the jury have found Lizzie Borden not guilty, given all of the evidence against her? According to Joseph Conforti, author of "Why 19th-Century Axe Murderer Lizzie Borden Was Found Not Guilty,"[39] the prosecution probably committed a cardinal sin. It underestimated its opponent.

Lizzie arrived for trial each day dressed appropriately in black since she was a young woman in mourning. She cinched in her waist with a corset and made sure to carry a bouquet of flowers and a fan to be deployed when the evidence was shocking or gruesome. In fact, when the state showed the victims' shattered skulls to the jury during the trial, Lizzie promptly fainted.

She did not look the part of a murderer. She was petite. If she was not strikingly pretty, she was at least not big-boned or coarse. She looked like a woman who had been raised by respectable people. She did not look like someone strong enough to cause the injuries inflicted on Andrew and Abby Borden, and she did not look like someone who would have been inclined to commit such a heinous crime.

Additionally, Lizzie had inherited her father's money, and this was no small thing. Among the lawyers she hired was a former governor of Massachusetts, the man who had appointed one of the three judges who presided over Lizzie's trial. That justice was the one who delivered the charge to the jury before it retired to deliberate, and many courtroom observers described the charge as quite favorable to the defense. The justice was also responsible for ruling against allowing the state to introduce evidence that Lizzie had purchased prussic acid.

Early on, the court had decided against including the citizens of Fall River on the jury itself. Therefore, the men who

---

[39] Joseph Conforti, "Why 19th-Century Axe Murderer Lizzie Borden Was Found Not Guilty," *Smithsonian Magazine* (July 23, 2019), https://www.smithsonianmag.com/history/why-19th-century-axe-murderer-lizzie-borden-was-found-not-guilty-180972707/.

were appointed to the jury came from the surrounding area, which was mostly agricultural. Many of them were fathers of daughters around Lizzie's age. It is possible that they simply could not imagine a young woman committing such a crime. It was learned later that they had quickly decided to acquit but waited an hour to report the decision to the court to avoid appearing reckless. Nevertheless, the prosecution had failed to meet its burden of proving guilt beyond a reasonable doubt. Lizzie went home to Fall River, where she lived until her death in 1927 at the age of sixty-seven.

CHAPTER FIVE

Ohio v. Sam Sheppard, December 21, 1954

The Sixth Amendment Right to a Fair Trial & the Due Process Clause of the Fourteenth Amendment[40]

IN "THE FUGITIVE," a television series and later a film, a man wrongfully accused of his wife's murder makes a daring run for it so he can prove his innocence. The story was loosely based on a real case, one in which the media coverage of a crime was intense and sensationalized. On July 3, 1954, the evening before the Fourth of July holiday, Dr. Sam Sheppard and his wife Marilyn were watching a movie with some friends in the Sheppards' home. The couple lived a comfortable life in Ohio, made possible by Sam's work as a neurosurgeon. Sam fell asleep during the evening, and Marilyn wished their friends a good night.

Sometime after that, Marilyn was bludgeoned to death in her bed. There was blood spatter all over the couple's bedroom and drops of blood on the floors around the house. A few small

---

[40] Douglas Linder, "Dr. Sam Sheppard Trials: An Account," famous-trials.com, https://famous-trials.com/sam-sheppard/2-sheppard.

items of jewelry, including Sam's watch and fraternity ring, were missing. Sometime later, they were located inside a bag hidden in some shrubs behind the house.

Sam told detectives that he had still been sleeping in the living room when he heard his wife screaming. He ran upstairs to the bedroom and saw what he thought was a man in the room but was then struck on the head and knocked unconscious. He came to in time to chase the person out of the house and onto the beach outside. Sam fought with the man but was knocked out again, and the man escaped. He awoke in the early morning hours and telephoned a neighbor for help. (The neighbor claimed Sam actually called him and asked him to come over because he thought he had killed his wife.)

The neighbor arrived a little before six in the morning. Sam was wearing no shirt, his pants were wet, and he had blood on his pants leg. When the police arrived a short time later, they noted that Sam seemed to be disoriented. The Sheppards' son, Chip, had slept through the night in an adjacent bedroom, and the neighbors had not heard the family's dog bark at any time.

The press went wild over the story. Not only were the local newspapers convinced that Sam was guilty, but they seemed to be engaged in gamesmanship with the police. On July 21, for example, the *Cleveland Press* ran an editorial calling for the coroner to hold a public inquest as soon as possible. Sure enough, within hours, the coroner scheduled the inquest to be held on the very next day. It was held in a school gymnasium, and people packed the stands to watch the proceedings. Sam's attorney was forced to sit with the crowd and not with his client. At one point, the attorney was forcibly removed from the building, and the crowd cheered. Nine days later, the paper demanded to know why Sam had not been arrested. Police arrested him that night.

The coverage itself was sensational but not necessarily well-grounded in fact. A local radio station claimed in one report that it had located Sam's "mistress," supposedly the mother of his illegitimate child. When an autopsy determined that Marilyn had been pregnant, there was speculation that she was carrying another man's child. Rumors of an affair between Sam and a nurse ran rampant. Sam denied that he had been unfaithful, but a woman, Susan Hayes, came forward to the police and claimed that she had been sleeping with him. The newspapers scoured the community for anyone willing to reveal more salacious details. A federal judge later said of the whole affair:

> "If ever there was a trial by newspaper, this is a perfect example. And the most insidious example was the Cleveland Press. For some reason that newspaper took upon itself the role of accuser, judge, and jury."

Sam finally went on trial in October 1954. His jury was not sequestered, meaning that they had the same access to newspapers and news reports as everyone else. Two of the jurors informed the court that they had heard the radio broadcast about Sam's supposed New York mistress, but the judge did not dismiss them from the jury. Several famous journalists attended the proceedings and wrote regular reports.

One of them was Dorothy Kilgallen, a star of the popular television show, "What's My Line?" She wrote a piece for syndication in which she compared Sam to Lizzie Borden. Although she did not report the conversation until much later, Kilgallen also overheard the judge, in his chambers, say that Sam was "guilty as hell." The judge denied defense motions to move or delay the trial because of the publicity. The names of the sitting jurors were published in the newspapers, meaning that the spotlight was now also glaringly focused on them. If they did not convict the defendant, the media would have something to say about it.

The state displayed gruesome autopsy photos to the jury. The coroner testified that he could make out, in the impression of a blood stain in Marilyn's bed, the impression of a surgical instrument. Despite the defense attorney's objection that this testimony was without foundation, the court allowed it to stand. Prosecutors also called Susan Hayes, the woman with whom Sam had been having an affair, and argued that the affair was Sam's motive for killing his wife. When the jury returned a guilty verdict, few were or could have been surprised. Sam was sentenced to life in prison.

Several appeals followed. None were successful until F. Lee Bailey took over the case. Bailey's petition for *habeas* relief was granted in 1964 in an opinion that called the trial a "mockery of justice." Sam was ordered to be released on bond, but in the meantime, the State of Ohio appealed. The case made its way to the Supreme Court, which struck down the conviction.

By that time, Dorothy Kilgallen had come forward to describe the statements she had heard the trial judge make, and his bias against the defendant was clear. The Court was troubled by the "carnival atmosphere" that had surrounded the proceedings thanks to media coverage and the judge's refusal to take any steps to mitigate the prejudice to the defendant that the ongoing coverage had caused. Sam would receive a new trial.

Jury selection in that case began in the fall of 1966. Newspapers and broadcasters continued to report from the trial, but this time the jury was sequestered. The new judge was careful to ensure there would be no more carnival in his courtroom. The coroner had a far less significant role, and he was not permitted to testify to his belief that an outline of a surgical instrument could be seen in a bloodstain. Susan Hayes was not

called as a witness. Instead, the evidence was much more focused on forensic science, particularly on how to interpret
blood spatters found at the scene and on a watch Sam was
wearing. Bailey, who continued to represent Sam, argued that
a woman might have killed Marilyn for having an affair with
her husband. Perhaps the most important difference in the evidence, though, is that Sam elected not to testify in his own
defense at his second trial, depriving the prosecution of the
chance to cross-examine him. He was acquitted.

CHAPTER SIX

California v. O.J. Simpson, October 3, 1995

The Sixth Amendment Right to a Fair Trial & the Due Process Clause of the Fourteenth Amendment [41]

THE LIZZIE BORDEN and Sam Sheppard trials were considered the celebrity trials of their time, and in the early nineteen-nineties, a similar trial captivated the United States. It involved a vicious killing, a beautiful woman, and beloved football player and movie actor, O.J. Simpson. Unlike those earlier trials, television would play a significant role. In fact, many people watched the proceedings play out live from the comfort of their living rooms. At 12:10 a.m. on June 13, 1994, Nicole Brown Simpson—O.J. Simpson's ex-wife—and her friend Ron Goldman were found stabbed to death outside Nicole's condominium in the Brentwood neighborhood of Los Angeles. O.J. was a member of the Pro Football Hall of Fame, a winner of the Heisman trophy, and he had appeared in small roles in a few films and in a series of television commercials. He was a

---

[41] Laura Shackel, "Case File: The OJ Simpson Trial," Forensic Science Society, https://forensicsciencesociety.com/thedrip/case-file-the-oj-simpson-trial.

well-known public figure and instantly recognizable to most people. So many were shocked when he quickly became a person of interest in the crime, owing to a bloody glove found behind his house. He was charged four days later.

Although he initially agreed to turn himself in voluntarily, O.J. apparently changed his mind, and for several hours he and his friend Al Cowlings, another former football player, led the police in a low-speed pursuit along a California freeway. Television studios covered the chase live, reporting from the ground in places along the route and from helicopters. Around 95 million people watched.

O.J. was finally taken into custody, but the publicity continued apace. A jury was sworn in for his trial in November 1994, and the trial took eleven months. Television cameras were permitted unprecedented access to the courtroom. CourtTV, a cable television channel, was launched in 1991 but found its niche with the Simpson case and another high-profile case, the murder trial of Eric and Lyle Menendez.

O.J. was represented by a team of respected and media-savvy lawyers. These included Johnnie Cochran, F. Lee Bailey (who had also represented Sam Sheppard), Alan Dershowitz, and Robert Kardashian. Barry Scheck, who has since become notable for his ties to the Innocence Project, joined the team and lent his expertise in a still relatively new field of forensics, DNA evidence.

The prosecutors included veteran lawyers William Hodgman, Marcia Clark, and a relatively green lawyer, Christopher Darden. Hodgman collapsed in the courtroom early on in the proceedings and was effectively replaced for the remainder of the trial by Darden. Darden and Cochran had been friends before the start of the trial, but their friendship would be severely tested. O.J., Cochran, and Darden were Black; most of the rest of the lawyers and most of the witnesses who would testify were white. Race would play a significant, controversial role in the case.

O.J.'s motive for the killings was, allegedly, domestic abuse in his marriage to Nicole Brown Simpson. He had pled guilty to domestic violence in 1989 before the couple divorced. The state claimed that on the night of June 12, 1994, O.J. spotted his ex-wife at a dance recital for their daughter and was furious that she was wearing a revealing dress. O.J. got home to find a message on his answering machine from his girlfriend, Paula Barbieri, breaking up with him. Supposedly he then drove to Nicole's condominium, hoping to reconcile with her but murdered her in a rage. Ron Goldman was killed because he happened upon the scene. Earlier in the day, Nicole's mother had left a pair of sunglasses at the restaurant where Ron was a food server, and he was attempting to return them.

In fact, the prosecution played for the jury a recording of a chilling phone call Nicole had made to 911 in January of 1989. Nicole could be heard pleading for help and stating that O.J. was going to harm her. O.J. could be heard in the background screaming, and there were sounds consistent with landing blows. An officer who responded to the call told the jury that Nicole emerged from bushes where she had been hiding and that she appeared bruised and battered. She told the detective that O.J. was going to kill her. Photos of Nicole's face from that night confirmed she had been beaten.

Another witness, Ron Shipp, a friend of O.J. and Nicole and an LAPD officer, told the jury that O.J. was worried about taking a polygraph and that he had been dreaming about killing his ex-wife. Nicole's sister testified that she had seen O.J. physically abusing Nicole—in one episode physically throwing her into a wall.

Several witnesses testified about facts that were key to establishing a timeline for the night of the murders. The medical examiner believed that Nicole had died sometime between 10:00 p.m. and 10:30 p.m. A friend of O.J.'s, Kato Kaelin, said that he saw O.J. at around 9:36 p.m. and then not again until 10:54 p.m. As a result, O.J. could not firmly establish where he had been during the crucial time period when the crimes were committed. Another witness, a limousine driver, testified that he had seen a figure resembling O.J. at the back of O.J.'s home that night, around the location where a bloody glove was recovered.

The prosecution claimed that O.J. returned home after the murders and then when he was seen by the limousine driver, panicked and went to the back of the house, where he dropped the glove. When he could not get in through the back door, he walked to the front of the house and entered that way.

The glove and other blood and DNA evidence were the focus of the case, as there were no eyewitnesses to the crime itself. Drops of blood or other DNA evidence were found in many areas, including in O.J.'s bedroom, near his car, on the glove, and on a pair of socks found in O.J.'s bedroom. Crime lab personnel also tied fibers found on the glove found at O.J.'s home to those found on a glove left at the crime scene and found hairs on the victims consistent with O.J.'s hair. Blue clothing fibers were left on the victims, and O.J. had worn a blue shirt to his daughter's dance recital that night, but the shirt he had been wearing disappeared and was never found. A shoe print expert testified that the killer had worn a pair of Bruno Magli loafers. These shoes, considered rare and extremely expensive, were sold at a department store where O.J. was known to shop. Only twenty-nine pairs of the shoes had been sold in the United States. O.J. wore size twelve shoes, the same size as the killer.

The prosecutors thought they had a very strong case. Cochran and the defense team, however, were able to poke holes in much of the state's evidence over the course of the trial. Questioning of evidence technicians and police personnel took weeks at a time. The defense was able to introduce doubt about the way the crime lab had processed evidence taken from the murder scene. Cochran, in particular, challenged the objectivity of the Los Angeles Police Department, suggesting that it was plagued by racism and incompetence. Detective Mark Fuhrman was forced to admit on the stand that he had used racist language at times. It was suggested that he had planted evidence, including the glove found at O.J.'s home.

Famously and disastrously for the prosecution, Darden suggested that O.J. try to put on the glove in open court. O.J., clearly aware that the jury and the country were watching, mugged and struggled, behaving as though the glove would not fit on his hand. Cochran, when he made his closing argument to the jury, uttered his famous epithet: "If it doesn't fit, you must acquit."

In October, O.J. was acquitted.

The country watched the trial in real-time with the jury. Opinions split along clear racial lines. Most Black people polled in Los Angeles County sided with the defense and considered the verdict justified by the evidence. White and Latino people sided overwhelmingly with the state and believed that the mostly Black jury had been swayed by race and not the evidence.

The trial had taken place in the shadow of the infamous Rodney King trial, following which riots had shaken Los Angeles. Officials were concerned that rioting would occur following the announcement of the verdict and increased police presence throughout the area, although their concerns proved unnecessary. Since the trial, the racial gap with respect to opinions about O.J.'s guilt has narrowed. A poll taken in 2013 indicated that more than fifty percent of Black respondents believed that O.J. had, in fact, murdered Nicole Brown Simpson and Ronald Goldman. Additionally, several years after the acquittal, the family of Ronald Goldman won a civil judgment against O.J. based on a jury's conclusion that he caused Ron and Nicole's deaths. The judgment remains unpaid.

CHAPTER SEVEN

Florida v. Casey Anthony, July 5, 2011

The Sixth Amendment Right to a Trial by an Impartial Jury[42]

FEW THINGS ARE more disturbing than the murder of a child. When a child is murdered by a parent, the community demands justice. Yet, on July 5, 2011, a jury found Casey Anthony not guilty of the murder and abuse of her three-year-old daughter, Caylee, whose body had been found in a trash bag in a forested area not far from Casey Anthony's parents' home.

It was a shocking end to a saga that began in June 2008, when Casey left her family's home along with Caylee and failed to return for a month. Casey's mother, Cindy Anthony, was in contact with Casey during that time and frequently asked about Caylee. Casey told her that she was busy with work or that Caylee was being cared for by a nanny. At some point, she claimed that Caylee had been kidnapped by the nanny.

---

[42] Tim Ott, "Casey Anthony: A Complete Timeline of Her Murder Case and Trial," (December 2, 2020), Biography.com, https://www.biography.com/news/casey-anthony-muder-trial-timeline-facts.

Casey's father, George Anthony, learned that his daughter's vehicle had been towed and impounded, and he traveled to the tow yard to claim it. When he did, however, he noted that the car smelled of decomposition; both he and a tow yard worker believed it was the odor of a dead body. Later, however, a bag of garbage was found in the car's trunk.

Unsatisfied with the information she was receiving from her daughter, Cindy Anthony reported Caylee missing on July 15, 2008. She told the 911 operator when she placed the call that she believed something was wrong and that Casey's vehicle smelled of decomposition. The Orange County Sheriff's Department opened an investigation.

Casey's story began falling apart immediately. Although she had claimed Caylee was with a nanny on various occasions during the preceding thirty-one days, detectives contacted the woman Casey identified, and she denied knowing the family. It became clear that there was no nanny.

Nor were there any pressing work assignments. Casey supposedly worked for Universal Studios, and in June of 2011, she had claimed to be too busy with work to bring Caylee to see her grandparents. Detectives learned that Casey hadn't worked at the theme park in several years. She had been lying about her employment to hide the fact that she had been fired. Casey's interactions with law enforcement were strange as well. She smiled and joked and was flirtatious; these behaviors were not consistent with the fact that her toddler was missing and unaccounted for.

She was arrested and charged with providing false statements to investigators, child neglect, and obstruction. After she spent a month in jail, a stranger posted bail for her in the hopes that she would lead investigators to Caylee's body. Casey, however, remained coy. In October, even though Caylee's body had not yet been recovered, Casey was indicted for first-degree murder, child abuse, and related charges. She was arrested again and this time held without bond. She pled not guilty.

In August of 2008, a local meter reader made several phone calls to the police to report a suspicious bag in a wooded area. An officer responded and searched the area but came away empty-handed. A few months later, the man called again. This time, a search team sadly recovered the remains of a small child placed in a trash bag. Also recovered from the scene was some duct tape attached to the child's hair and, eventually, bones scattered around the area. The medical examiner determined that the remains belonged to Caylee Anthony and determined that she had died as a result of homicide. However, the cause of her death could not be determined.

Prosecutors announced that they would seek the death penalty. The trial of Casey Anthony began in May 2011 and lasted six weeks. During that time, because of the significant media coverage of the crime, the jury was sequestered and instructed to avoid media and reports about the case.

The evidence against Casey was largely circumstantial. It included a strand of hair found in the trunk of Casey's car that was similar to hair taken from Caylee's hairbrush. An expert testified that there was "root-banding" on the hair, suggesting that the person had died before the hair was lost. The meter reader, whose calls to the police tip line led to the discovery of Caylee's remains, testified as well.

The smell associated with Casey's car was an important piece of evidence. An expert told the jury that he took air samples from the vehicle and found chemical compounds consistent with decomposition. The expert also found chloroform in the trunk. This was significant because prosecutors claimed that Casey had searched the Internet for information about chloroform and how to break a person's neck before Caylee's disappearance.

Additional physical evidence linked Casey to her daughter's remains. A blanket found in the wooded area matched a bedding set kept at Cindy and George's home. Casey had dated a man who kept a photo on his computer in which a man incapacitated a woman with chloroform.

Casey's attorneys deployed an aggressive and controversial defense. They claimed that Caylee had accidentally drowned in her grandparents' swimming pool in June; that her grandfather, George Anthony, found her body; and that he and Casey worked together to cover up Caylee's death to ensure that Casey would not be charged with neglecting the child. This, the attorneys said, was why Casey had behaved so strangely in the days after the child went missing. She knew Caylee was dead, and she was actively in denial. The attorneys alleged that Casey had been sexually abused by her father and that she had developed these behaviors as a result of this trauma. They even challenged the credibility of the man who had found Caylee's remains, suggesting that he might have moved the bones from one location to the one in which they were found in order to implicate Casey.

The jury acquitted Casey Anthony of the most serious charges against her. She was found guilty of providing false information to law enforcement. Given the amount of time she had already been held during trial, she was released from jail after only a few more weeks.

One of the jurors later spoke about how the verdict still impacted him nearly ten years later. "I think now if I were to do it over again, I'd push harder to convict her of one of the lesser charges like aggravated manslaughter," he told *People Magazine.* "At least that. Or child abuse. I didn't know what the hell I was doing, and I didn't stand up for what I believed in at the time."[43]

---

[43] Emma Hernandez, "Casey Anthony Now: Where She Is After the Death of Her Daughter," (October 3, 2022), intouchweekly.com, https://www. intouchweekly.com/posts/where-is-casey-anthony-now-see-where-she-is-after-the-death-of-her-daughter/.

CHAPTER EIGHT

Defining the Boundaries

"Independence means you decide according to the law and the facts." [44]

THE PRECEDING CASES, which span more than a century, are just a few of the high-profile criminal cases in which defendants were acquitted of the charges levied against them despite overwhelming evidence as a result of the rights and protections afforded to them, and indeed to all citizens. These rights were held sacred by the Founding Fathers.

Many consider these cases miscarriages of justice. Examined from the macro level, they exemplify the premise upon which our justice system is based: that it is better to preserve the rights of the guilty than to risk the conviction of the innocent. It is better that 100 guilty people go free than for one innocent person to be convicted of a crime.

This concept becomes even more evident and—to many—infuriating when issues of policing and race are brought into play. Criminal prosecutions, especially those involving deaths caused by police officers, have in recent years led to protests and, in some cases, rioting.

---

[44] Justice Stephen Breyer (1994–2022).

Appellate courts continually define the boundaries of our constitutional protections as guidance for the trial courts and law enforcement officers who carry out activities necessary to our criminal justice system.

But what about the impact of these boundaries?

The boundaries developed by the Supreme Court are outer limit boundaries, meant to show how far police can go before crossing the line into a Constitutional violation.

But as we will see in the next section, these boundaries are continually tested by local governing authorities across the country. In many ways, this exercise has become a political one with dire consequences.

PART THREE

DISPARITIES IN JUSTICE

"[T]he criminal is to go free because the constable has blundered[?]"
—**Benjamin Cardozo**, New York Court of Appeals Judge (1914-1932)
and later Supreme Court Justice (1932-1938)
People v. Defore, 242 N.Y. 13 (1926)

"The criminal goes free, if he must, but it is the law that sets him free."
—**Tom C. Clark**, Supreme Court Justice (1949-1967)
Mapp v. Ohio, 367 U.S. 643 (1961)

CHAPTER NINE

The Broken Windows Theory

"If children do not understand the Constitution,
they cannot understand how our government functions,
or what their rights and responsibilities are as citizens
of the United States." [45]

THE BROKEN WINDOWS THEORY of law enforcement was introduced in 1982 by two social scientists in an article published in *Atlantic Monthly*.[46] They theorized that visible signs of crime and disorder in a community encourage further crime, including more serious kinds of crime.

The name for this theory, Broken Windows, derives from the idea that once a window is broken and left that way, it sends a message that the property doesn't matter. If the window is broken, there's no reason to fix the roof. Once the roof is damaged, there's little reason to tend to the garden. Gradually, the house sinks into ruin, and so goes the neighborhood. Community residents take this to heart. As the area becomes

---

[45] Chief Justice John G. Roberts, Jr. (2005–present).

[46] George Kelling and James Wilson, "Broken Windows," The *Atlantic Monthly* (March 1982), https://www.theatlantic.com/magazine/archive/1982/03/broken-windows/304465/.

less appealing, crime rates rise.

When something like this happens, the theory continues, the neighborhood becomes a good place for teens skipping school to hang out. Panhandlers take up spots on the sidewalk. Prostitutes take to the streets, along with narcotics dealers and their customers. Residents frightened of or disgusted with this state of affairs either move away or stay inside their homes. This, in turn, only leads to more criminal activity in public spaces. Formerly non-violent crimes such as theft become violent crimes.

According to the article, fixing broken windows sends the message that even minor crimes will not be tolerated. To offer another analogy, if you clean up the trash and debris on the sidewalks in your neighborhood every day, people are less likely to litter. When these minor issues are tended to, more serious issues seem unthinkable.

Applied to policing as it was, Broken Windows encouraged law enforcement to target minor crimes such as public intoxication, vandalism, loitering, jaywalking, and even riding bicycles on the sidewalk. This approach, according to the theorists, would ensure an environment of general law and order. Knowing that minor crimes would be prosecuted would minimize or even prevent more serious crimes.

Terry & *Wardlow*: Wide Latitude Given

As promising as the Broken Windows approach to policing seemed to be, it had to contend with Constitutional limitations. Politicians can only go so far in instructing the police, no matter how supportive the voters may seem to be. Preventing the commission of minor crimes may have been the mandate, but police officers were still required to have probable cause to believe that a crime was occurring or would soon occur before they could make a stop.

Probable cause requires more than mere suspicion. It also does not require as much information as would be required to prove a suspect guilty beyond a reasonable doubt.

How much information do police officers need to justify a warrantless arrest? How much do they need to conduct a stop-and-frisk? What level of suspicion is required before police may enter a high-crime neighborhood to sweep for open warrants, contraband, or criminal activity?

Terry v. Ohio[47] and *Illinois v. Wardlow*[48] were decided to answer many of these questions. Both decisions expanded the latitude granted to the police for performing stop-and-frisks. Additionally, police officers have traditionally been allowed to make searches incident to an arrest of a suspect, no matter how minor the suspect's underlying crime might be. This was justified by the need to ensure that suspects were not armed. These searches often turn up evidence of other crimes.

Terry requires that a police officer have only a "reasonable and articulable suspicion" that a crime is being or is about to be committed; if so, the officer may stop the suspect for a brief encounter in order to dispel the officer's suspicions. During the stop, the officer can pat down the detainee to check for weapons for safety during the encounter. And if the officer can tell, based upon the plain feel of the object, that the suspect is carrying contraband, the officer may remove and seize the contraband, whether it be drugs, guns, or the like.

The Supreme Court elaborated on the meaning of "reasonable and articulable suspicion" in *Wardlow*. The Court said that the concept of reasonable and articulable suspicion must take into account the totality of the circumstances. This means that the character of the neighborhood where the stop itself

---

[47] *Terry*, 392 U.S. at 1.

[48] *Wardlow*, 528 U.S. at 119.

takes place is relevant. If a stop takes place within an area known for high-crime rates or for certain kinds of crime, such as the drug trade, law enforcement may take this into consideration in deciding whether to make a stop. Additionally, as in *Wardlow*, the mere fact that a person runs away from a police officer may be relevant to the inquiry.

This means that if the police see you drinking publicly, loitering, littering, jaywalking, or even riding a bicycle on a sidewalk against a city ordinance, they have the authority to arrest, search, and charge you. Before the advent of the Broken Windows policing era, though, officers rarely exercised this authority. They might issue you a citation or a warning. They might tell you to take your bicycle and go home. But they probably would not have arrested you. After Broken Windows, and with the support of politicians, law enforcement undertook to utilize arrests for even minor offenses as a way to reduce crime. However, the costs of this new approach were significant. You need only look to the City of Baltimore to see what happened.

Baltimore, MD: A Study in Constitutional Rights

I had recently moved to Baltimore from the New York City area to begin my first semester at the University of Maryland School of Law. A movement was sweeping the country, inspired by Broken Windows and the tremendous reduction in crime achieved by then-Mayor Rudy Giuliani. A local politician, a graduate of the very law school I was attending, was generating his own buzz based on a similar approach to law enforcement.

In Baltimore,[49] a Democratic stronghold, the general election

---

[49] Baltimore City is distinct from Baltimore County. They have their own governments, their own school systems, their own police forces. Confusion

is a fait accompli. The battle occurs at the primary election level. Whoever pulls off a victory in the Democratic Primary in the city is usually a shoo-in to win the respective office in the general election. Martin O'Malley had just won the Democratic mayoral primary.

After a sweeping victory, O'Malley took office in 1999, promising a massive reduction in crime in one of America's most dangerous and violent cities. He planned to follow the Rudy Giuliani model of crime reduction in New York City, and Giuliani used the Broken Windows model. On that basis, New York City police officers were making frequent stop-and-frisks in neighborhoods to send the message that no crime, no matter how minor, would be tolerated.

Baltimore was poised to seat a new mayor and initiate a new era of policing and law enforcement. It would take nearly twenty years for the impact of these policies on the community to become clear, and by then, the seeds of distrust and disunity would be very deeply sown. As a Baltimore prosecutor in 2003 with "boots on the ground," I was a first-hand witness to the impact of the policing theory on the justice system I was sworn to protect.

So why did O'Malley believe that Broken Windows would be successful in Baltimore? For sure, he had seen the apparently positive results in New York. There, the crime rates for felonies and misdemeanors fell significantly once Broken Windows was implemented, and they continued falling for ten straight years. Broken Windows seemed to be effective and long-lasting. This staying power proved to be a huge problem once the theory's shortcomings were revealed.

In 1985, the New York City Transit Authority hired George Kelling as a consultant. Kelling was one of the authors of the

---

has often resulted because people refer to one or the other simply as "Baltimore." For the purposes of this discussion, "Baltimore" means "Baltimore City."

Atlantic Monthly article and a key figure in the development of the theory. The Transit Authority began by removing graffiti in the subway system. When William Bratton subsequently became head of the Transit Authority Police, he continued implementing Kelling's theory by taking tougher stances on fare jumping and other minor crimes. He also ordered background checks on all who were arrested, leading to further prosecutions where arrestees were on probation or if other warrants were outstanding.

When Rudy Giuliani became mayor in 1993, he named William Bratton the City's Police Commissioner. He directed Bratton to bring his Broken Windows policies with him. Bratton was happy to do so. He directed City police to strictly enforce laws against transit fare evasion, drinking in public, urinating in public, and other petty crimes. Supposedly these sorts of offenses had a negative effect on life in the communities where they were being committed.

O'Malley believed the same problems existed in Baltimore's troubled communities. If so, they could be ameliorated with the same kind of hardline policing. During his first term in office, O'Malley directed his police commissioner to implement Broken Windows in Baltimore. During a political speech in 2015, O'Malley reflected on his time in office during the early aughts:

> *(In 1999), Baltimore had become the most violent, the most addicted and the most abandoned city in America. The biggest enemy that we faced was not the drug dealers or crack cocaine. It was a lack of belief. ... We started setting goals with deadlines and instead of simply setting goals with inputs, as government always does, we started measuring outputs. ... When the people of Baltimore saw their government was working again, they rallied, too. Together, we put into action that powerful belief, that in our city, there is no such thing as a spare American. That*

we're all in this together. And over the next 10 years, Baltimore went on to achieve the biggest reduction in Part 1 crime[50] in any major city in America.[51]

As Michelle Ye Hee Lee reported in the *Washington Post*,[52] Baltimore's crime rates did fall. Between 1999 and 2009, they fell by roughly forty-eight percent, an enormous reduction. For the often-demoralized City Police Department, it represented a needed win and permitted the department to claim the largest reduction in crime in the country for that time. The city that had been, in 1999, the single most violent, crime-ridden place in the country dropped, by 2009, to thirteenth on the list.

The homicide rate, considered an important indicator by many criminologists, dropped to its lowest level in years. Perhaps tellingly, however, the overall rate remained high in comparison to other United States cities. Baltimore was ranked second on the list of large cities—places like Chicago, Los Angeles, and New York City—based on its number of homicides.

The Broken Windows approach meant many, many more arrests. By 2005, as O'Malley was beginning his second mayoral term, the Baltimore Police Department had arrested so many people that courtrooms were literally overflowing with them. The Sixth Amendment, as we reviewed in a previous chapter, requires that governments provide speedy trials

---

[50] Part 1 crimes are serious crimes that are likely to be reported to police. They include things like homicide, forcible rape, robbery, aggravated assault, arson, and motor vehicle theft.

[51] Michelle Ye Hee Lee, "O'Malley's claim about crime rates in Baltimore," The *Washington Post* (Apr. 28, 2015), https://www.washingtonpost.com/news/fact-checker/wp/2015/04/28/omalleys-claim-about-crime-rates-in-baltimore/.

[52] *Id.*

to people who are charged with crimes. Speedy trials in Baltimore were virtually impossible. There were simply too many defendants and too few judges and courtrooms available. As a result, many of the people who were arrested had to be released. An absurd percentage of the total Baltimore population—more than sixteen percent—were arrested, and about two-thirds of people in jail at any one time were there for non-violent offenses.

All these things considered, Broken Windows reduced the crime rate in Baltimore, although the homicide rate remained high, and led to significant slowdowns within the court and carceral systems. It may not yet be possible to gauge whether Broken Windows was, therefore, a net improvement for safety within the community, which was its purpose. What is clear is that Broken Windows significantly and negatively impacted the communities it was designed to serve. Tensions between residents and the police department grew. The relationship, frankly, broke down.

As former Maryland Lieutenant Governor Michael Steele, a law and order Republican, put it:

> Go back to 2005, 2006 when then-Mayor O'Malley had a policy in place where everything was on lockdown. You couldn't sit on your stoop, people were harassed, and so all these tensions have been building and simmering for some time.[53]

In fact, as early as November 2005, some state lawmakers were becoming frustrated with the city's stop-and-frisk protocols. According to Maryland State Delegate Jill Carter: "These

---

[53] Ben Schreckinger, "O'Malley returns home to tough questions," Politico.com (Apr. 28, 2015), https://www.politico.com/story/2015/04/martin-omalley-returns-home-to-tough-questions-117454.

are Gestapo tactics, all in a mad rush to get crime down, and it isn't working."[54] In a piece that appeared on CBS News that year, the author wrote: "Even patrol officers complained to their union representatives that the stop-and-frisk tactic was overused ... Some officers reportedly called stop-and-frisks a 'VCR detail,' abbreviated for 'violation of civil rights.'"[55]

In 2012, the Baltimore City Police Department surveyed residents about their satisfaction with the department.[56] When it came to specific questions about "preventing crime" or "professionalism," fewer than half were satisfied. Only in one category out of five—namely, "police presence"—did more than fifty percent of residents say they were satisfied. There were plenty of officers on the streets.

Very troublingly, the approach seems to have been discriminatory from the outset. Officers looking for people with outstanding warrants or who might be carrying contraband targeted neighborhoods that were mostly Black. They stopped and patted down thousands of people simply because those people were Black and living in Black neighborhoods. Many believed that this amounted to an ongoing violation of the Fourteenth Amendment's equal protection clause.[57]

---

[54] Stephanie Condon, "Did Martin O'Malley's criminal justice policies help or hurt Baltimore?" CBS News (May 6, 2015), https://www.cbsnews.com/news/did-martin-omalleys-criminal-justice-policies-help-hurt-baltimore/.

[55] *Id.*

[56] 2012 Citizen Survey Report for PoliceStat, https://bbmr.baltimorecity.gov/sites/default/files/Policestat%202012-%201_8_13.pdf.

[57] As described in a section below, the City of Baltimore would later settle a lawsuit filed by the U.S. Department of Justice (DOJ) for racially discriminatory policing procedures. Baltimore City Consent Decree, U.S. District Court for the District of Maryland, https://www.mdd.uscourts.gov/Baltimore-City-Consent-Decree.

Prosecution Policies and the Judiciary

Baltimore has two levels of trial courts to deal with the massive number of arrests making their way into the judicial system. The district court is the first-line court, where misdemeanors and small civil claims are tried solely by judges. A defendant who wants a jury trial must request one, and then the case will be transferred to the circuit court, which is the trial court of general jurisdiction, hearing all kinds of cases. Prosecutors recently graduated from law school are generally assigned to work in the district court, where they can learn the ins and outs of trying cases before they begin working in the circuit court. I was no different.

During my tenure there, I was calling dockets of thirty or more cases every other day in the district court. This was the height of the O'Malley stop-and-frisk, zero tolerance, Broken Windows era. I distinctly remember being chastised in open court one morning by a judge who could more readily see what was happening in the community. Judge Nathan Braverman looked at me and said:

> "Mr. Oberer, what are you doing? Why are you prosecuting all of these people for these nothing offenses? You are prosecuting citizens that were shaken down by the police; you are prosecuting them into having a criminal record. And for what, drinking in public, loitering, urinating on a lamppost? Are you serious? Don't you see...when you get to the circuit court, these are going to be the very people that are pooled to be on your jury for more serious crimes. Do you know how many convictions these folks are going to return?!?!—NONE!!!"

But what was I supposed to do? I was hired to do this job. I remember feeling frustrated—not at Judge Braverman, who, by all accounts, was a judge that really got it; he cared about the people who appeared before him and did fabulous work. I was frustrated because I knew he was right. I knew that there were only so many people who could be brought in to serve as jurors, that it was going to be hard to find twelve people able to serve who had not been involved with one of these run-ins with the police, and that dangerous and violent criminals charged with more serious crimes were going to walk because of it. I told the court:

> *"Yes, your Honor. I understand your point. I hear what you are saying. You are wiser than I. But I am obligated to pursue these cases as legitimately charged crimes. I do not have the discretion to simply tell the police department that I decline to enforce the law by dropping the cases they are bringing me. That's the policy of our office. I have not made it down to the circuit court yet to select juries and try cases before them to see this impact."*

But I soon would. And I would see the calamitous effects of prosecuting so many low-level Broken Windows cases against people who would soon be on my juries.

Judge Braverman was right. Not only were these policies making it difficult to try violent criminals, but they were also feeding the community's anger and frustration, and that anger and frustration were about to reach a precipitous threshold. There would be a backlash. In fact, there would be two major backlashes in Baltimore: riots sparked by two major police-involved incidents followed by a Department of Justice consent decree.

The Impact on the Citizens and the Courts

Broken Windows gave the police pretty much *carte blanche* to stop and frisk. Courts, bound by *Terry* and *Wardlow*, could do very little about it. The policy was a political one, and for a time, it was popular with many voters.

It had its share of critics. Some considered it nothing more than a fishing expedition, permitting police to enter high-crime neighborhoods to search for people who "looked" like criminals. (That "look" often had much to do with race.) Police officers then only needed a "reasonably articulable suspicion" under *Terry* or *Wardlow* to stop and frisk people. Those reasons were easy to find; if you're a cynical person, you might wonder whether reasons were often "found" well after an arrest had already been made. So long as an officer's stop was reasonable, the officer could search for contraband and run the suspect's name through open warrant databases, hoping for a hit.

However many actual criminals Broken Windows had plucked from the streets, it also netted many, *many* innocent, law-abiding citizens who were doing nothing more than living in a crime-affected neighborhood when they were shaken down. These citizens felt, with good reason, that they had been stopped because they were Black. Prosecutors were asking these people to serve as impartial jurors even though much of the testimony they would be asked to hear would be delivered by the police officers who were harassing them and their communities. The situation was impossible. It soon exploded.

The Aftermath and Riots

After nearly a decade of zero-tolerance law enforcement in Baltimore, people grew wary of constant police presence. The death of Freddie Gray ripened weariness into anger and even hatred.

Freddie Gray was twenty-five years old on the morning of April 12, 2015. He lived in Gilmor Homes, a housing project in the West Baltimore neighborhood of Sandtown-Winchester. Like many public housing communities, Gilmor's residents were mostly Black. Drugs were sold openly on the street, and violent crimes occurred with frequency.

The city's recently elected State's Attorney, Marilyn Mosby, had charged the Baltimore Police Department with increased drug enforcement work at the corner of West North Avenue and North Mount Street. Early that morning, three officers— Lieutenant Brian W. Rice, Officer Edward Nero, and Officer Garrett E. Miller—laid eyes on Gray. Gray began to run. This, as in *Wardlow*, suggested to the officers that Gray was up to no good, and therefore they gave chase.

Once he was apprehended, the officers found a small knife clipped to the inside of his front pants pocket. It was a switchblade, the possession of which is illegal in Baltimore and most cities across the country. Gray was cuffed and loaded into a "wagon," the van used for transporting arrestees to the jail pending arraignment. He was not seat belted. Some alleged that he was then, possibly, given a "rough ride"—an unsanctioned police practice in which an unsecured prisoner is driven erratically. The wagon made several confirmed stops, and during one stop, Gray was placed in leg irons. Another stop was made at a grocery store. Yet another stop was made in order to load another prisoner into the van.

The officers reached their destination, the Western District police station, at a little more than twenty minutes past nine in the morning. Gray was non-responsive. Paramedics were summoned and attempted to revive him. He was then rushed to Shock Trauma, where he was found to be comatose. Efforts were made to save his life over the next few days. He had several fractured vertebrae in his neck, and his spinal cord had been almost completely severed. He died on April 19, 2015, one week after he had been arrested.

Gray's death had not occurred in a vacuum. His death was

preceded by the deaths of Trayvon Martin, Michael Brown, Sandra Bland, and others at the hands of police or otherwise as a result of law enforcement failures. Many felt that Gray seemed to be yet another victim of bad or racist policing. Hundreds of people gathered outside the headquarters of the Baltimore Police Department in April. On April 22, 2015, Gene Ryan, then-President of the Fraternal Order of Police, issued a statement criticizing the protestors and suggesting that they resembled a lynch mob. Given that lynch mobs were generally mobilized to victimize Black people, not to empower them, these words were ill-considered at best and cruel at worst. They only enraged the protestors further.

On April 25, 2015, protests in downtown Baltimore turned violent. Members of the crowd threw rocks at the lines of police officers facing them, outfitted in riot gear and carrying shields and pepper spray. Fires were set in several businesses. More than thirty people were arrested, and fifteen officers were injured. The situation grew worse two days later following Gray's funeral. Protestors began looting. Two police cruisers were destroyed. A pharmacy was set on fire.

Maryland Governor Larry Hogan declared a state of emergency and sent in state troopers and members of the Army National Guard to restore order. Tensions remained high for weeks, with breakouts of sporadic episodes of looting or sparring. The National Guard finally began withdrawing from Baltimore on May 3, 2015. The curfew was lifted. Residents began to catch their breath.

The Federal Consent Decree

United States Attorney General Loretta Lynch announced five days later that the Department of Justice would undertake a review of the City Police Department on account of the "serious erosion of public trust" in relation to Gray's death.

Members of the Justice Department's Civil Rights Division searched for evidence of police brutality, excessive force, or regularly engaging in discriminatory police practices. They found it.

The information uncovered by the DOJ as part of its investigation suggested that the Baltimore Police Department began disproportionately targeting African-American people for stops and arrests shortly after the department unveiled its zero-tolerance approach in the early 2000s.[58] The scathing report left little room for debate that the department was engaged in a pattern of discriminatory law enforcement behavior.

But there was some room for debate, and critics made the most of it. Some argued that it would be hard for police not to target Black people in a city that is sixty-three percent Black, and where of the 211 homicides committed in 2014, eighty percent occurred within a small number of high-poverty, Black neighborhoods. According to an October 6, 2016, report in the *Baltimore Sun*,[59] around eighty percent of the city's gun homicides are committed in twenty-five percent of the city's neighborhoods. Those neighborhoods are predominantly African-American. Critics also pointed out that stepped-up policing in neighborhoods relatively unaffected by crime would be a poor use of limited police resources and that law enforcement cannot change the demographic makeup of neighborhoods.

According to statistics analyzed in the DOJ report, the magnitude of racial differences in stops, searches, and arrests

---

[58] Justice Department Announces Findings of Investigation into Baltimore Police Department (Aug. 10, 2016), https://www.justice.gov/opa/pr/justice-department-announces-findings-investigation-baltimore-police-department.

[59] Justin George, "Baltimore emergency rooms struggle to care for severely wounded patients," The *Baltimore Sun* (Oct. 14, 2016), https://www.baltimoresun.com/news/investigations/bal-shoot-to-kill-part-three-story.html.

is so pronounced that it is reasonable to conclude that intentional discrimination is at work. Investigators found instances in which officers were ordered to directly target Black residents. In one case, a commander allegedly gave an order to "lock up all the Black hoodies."

The statistics demonstrated that the Baltimore Police Department stopped and arrested more people in predominantly Black areas of the city. From January 2010 through May 2014, police made some 300,000 stops—forty-four percent of which were in two predominantly Black areas that make up twelve percent of the city's population.

Citywide, the report found, the Baltimore Police Department "stopped African-American residents three times as often as white residents after controlling for the population of the area in which the stops occurred." The report states:

> Starting in at least the late 1990s ... City and BPD leadership responded to the City's challenges by encouraging 'zero tolerance' street enforcement that prioritized officers making large numbers of stops, searches, and arrests—and often resorting to force—with minimal training and insufficient oversight from supervisors or through other accountability structures. These practices led to repeated violations of the constitutional and statutory rights, further eroding the community's trust in the police. BPD's legacy of zero tolerance enforcement continues to drive its policing in certain Baltimore neighborhoods and leads to unconstitutional stops, searches, and arrests. Many BPD supervisors instruct officers to make frequent stops and arrests—even for minor offenses and with minimal or no suspicion—without sufficient consideration of whether this enforcement strategy promotes public safety and community trust or conforms to constitutional standards. These instructions, coupled with

minimal supervision and accountability for misconduct, lead to constitutional violations.

The DOJ's investigation led to negotiations and an eventual agreement with the Baltimore Police Department that was designed to curb some of the violations found. This type of agreement, known as a consent decree, requires stringent record-keeping and the appointment of an independent monitor responsible for ensuring that the agreement is actually implemented.

On April 7, 2017, Chief Judge James K. Bredar of the United States District Court for the District of Maryland approved the consent decree. The agreement calls for a wide range of police reforms, including improved training, new technology, and community oversight. During the year the consent decree was approved, Baltimore saw a more than sixty-three percent increase in homicides, from 211 homicides in 2014 to 342 homicides in 2017.[60]

"Zero Tolerance" Implementation

As of 2019, six major U.S. cities—New York, Chicago, Los Angeles, Boston, Baltimore, and Denver—had employed some version of the Broken Windows theory in their policing tactics, stressing aggressive enforcement of minor misdemeanor laws.[61]

Baltimore's experience is not unique. In 2013, the Vera Institute of Justice reported that the application of the theory in

---

[60] "Baltimore Homicides," The *Baltimore Sun*, https://homicides.news.baltimoresun.com/. *See also* John Gramlich, "What we know about the increase in U.S. murders in 2020," Pew Research Center.

[61] Robert Longley, "What Is the Broken Windows Theory?" ThoughtCo. (July 03, 2019), https://www.thoughtco.com/broken-windows-theory-46 85946.

New York had similarly destroyed trust between residents of policed neighborhoods and the police.[62] The organization surveyed 500 young people and found that only around forty percent would approach a police officer if they were in trouble. Nearly ninety percent of survey respondents indicated that the people in their communities no longer trusted police officers.

---

[62] Stephanie Condon, "Did Martin O'Malley's criminal justice policies help or hurt Baltimore?" CBS News (May 6, 2015), https://www.cbsnews.com/ news/did-martin-omalleys-criminal-justice-policies-help-hurt-baltimore/. Recalibrating Justice: A Review of 2013 State Sentencing and Corrections Trends, Vera Institute of Justice, https://www.vera.org/publications/ state-sentencing-and-corrections-trends-2013.

CHAPTER TEN

Civil Unrest:
When Citizens Retaliate
Against Unjust Policing Tactics

"There is no such thing as justice—in or out of court." [63]

TENSIONS BETWEEN POLICE AND civilians are nothing new. The perception that our criminal justice system is designed to find the truth, provide recourse, and offer fairness has occasionally sparked anger and rage. Factor in racism and discrimination as underlying reasons for particular incidents of alleged police brutality and misconduct, and many Americans will react with civil unrest, death, and destruction.

The "injustice" of the justice system has led to a buildup of frustration and anger, hopelessness and helplessness, often culminating in violence and riots.

Such incidents date back to the earliest days of the country. The American Revolution, for example, began with an act of civil disobedience. This discussion will begin, however, with the 1960s and, in particular, with the Civil Rights Movement. Historically, police officers have been given wide latitude

---

[63] Clarence Darrow (American Defense Attorney (1857–1938)).

within which to act, and that latitude has often resulted in officers not being held accountable. Recently, there is evidence that the tide has turned. Technology—namely cell phones with video capability and officer-worn body cameras—is now capable of recording what officers do in real-time.

Even when police officers are charged with crimes committed within the scope of their duties, the state must prove the charges beyond a reasonable doubt with admissible evidence, or acquittals will result. Law enforcement officers are afforded the same constitutional rights as every other citizen of this country. The failure to understand this underlying scheme, in which the rights of defendants outweigh other interests, including the public's interest in achieving justice, has led to instances of civil unrest.

Harlem Riots, 1964 [64]

In July of 1964, a fifteen-year-old African-American boy, James Powell, was shot and killed by a New York City police officer in front of several of Powell's friends and other eyewitnesses. Powell and some other young Black men had been hanging around in a mostly white, working-class neighborhood on the Upper East Side of Manhattan. According to reports, in an effort to force them out of the neighborhood, a man sprayed the boys with a garden hose and yelled insults. Powell and the other young men responded by throwing garbage and garbage can lids back. Then Powell chased the man into an apartment building. Powell was inside the building for only a minute or two.

When he stepped out, he was immediately confronted by

---

[64] "Disasters: New York City (NYC) Harlem Riots of 1964," https://www.baruch.cuny.edu/nycdata/disasters/riots-harlem_1964.html.

an off-duty police officer, Lieutenant Thomas Gilligan. Gilligan had been in a nearby shop when the initial altercation occurred. For reasons that remain unclear, Gilligan drew his service weapon and shot Powell three times. It is unclear whether Gilligan fired his shots in rapid succession or if time passed between them. It is also unclear whether Powell was in possession of a knife. Some witnesses believed that an ambulance called to attend to Powell took an unusually long time to respond and that Powell might have survived his wounds had he been helped more quickly.

This evidence was presented to a grand jury. The grand jury declined to indict Gilligan. The grand jury's failure to indict led to rioting that occurred over six nights in Harlem and Bedford-Stuyvesant. There were incidents of vandalism and looting, as well as attacks on members of the police department. A number of protestors were subjected to police beatings. One rioter was killed, 118 were injured, and 465 were arrested.

Tampa Race Riots, 1967 [65]

Rioting also took place in Tampa, Florida, during "the long, hot summer of 1967."[66] Tensions were sparked when police

---

[65] Paul Guzzo, "Racism in Tampa boiled over 50 years ago into Central Avenue riots," *Tampa Bay Times* (Jun. 8, 2017), https://www.tampabay .com/news/humaninterest/racism-in-tampa-boiled-over-50-years-ago- into-central-avenue-riots/2326360/.

[66] *See also* Buffalo riots of 1967 (June 26–July 1); Cambridge riots of 1967 (July 24, 1967); Cincinnati riots of 1967 (June 12–June 15); Detroit riots of 1967 (July 23–28); Milwaukee riots of 1967 (July 30–August 3); Minneapolis riots of 1967 (July 20–21); Newark riots of 1967 (July 12–17); Plainfield riots of 1967 (July 14–16); Portland riots of 1967 (July 30); Saginaw riots of 1967 (July 26); and Toledo riots of 1967 (July 23–25).

killed a nineteen-year-old Black man, Martin Chambers, in the Central Park Village neighborhood. At the time, Central Park Village was the largest Black neighborhood in the area.

Tampa police believed that Chambers and two other men had robbed a camera supply store. Police officers shot and killed him when he attempted to flee. The officers said they shot Chambers because otherwise, he would have escaped, yet that was not a basis for the use of deadly force under these circumstances or the law.

Peaceful protests began that afternoon and became violent by evening. The rioting lasted three days and came to an end only when the governor ordered members of the National Guard, state troopers, and other local law enforcement officers to assist in clearing the streets. By the end of the episode, more than 100 people had been arrested, and $2 million in damage had been done to property.

The district attorney's office completed a cursory investigation that lasted only two days. No charges were filed due to what was said to be insufficient evidence.

Camden, New Jersey Riots, 1971 [67]

The Camden, New Jersey riots of 1971 followed the death of Rafael Rodriguez Gonzalez, a Puerto Rican man, while in police custody. The officers responsible claimed that Gonzalez was subdued because he was resisting arrest.

Racial tensions in Camden were already high. Three years before, a group of mostly Black residents gathered outside of Cooper University Hospital in response to a rumor that a

---

[67] Alfonso A. Narvaez, "1 Killed, 2 Shot in Camden Riots," The *New York Times* (Aug. 22, 1971), https://www.nytimes.com/1971/08/22/archives/1-killed-2-shot-in-camden-riots-mayor-declares-emergency-after-2d.html.

white police officer had beaten a Black child. A sniper fired a shot into the crowd, killing one woman and an officer. The shooter was never apprehended. Rioting occurred over the following days in a town that had already been decimated by white flight and economic decline.

When news of Gonzalez's death spread, members of the local Hispanic community demanded justice. Camden's mayor initially ignored this, and as a result, residents again began to riot. Fires were set. Eighty-seven people were injured, and 300 arrests were made. Finally, the police officers who had arrested Gonzalez were charged with battery and then murder. The officers were acquitted of the most serious charges; however, they were finally convicted of manslaughter.

Queens, New York Riots, 1973 [68]

The death of Clifford Glover, a ten-year-old boy, set off rioting in Queens in 1973. Again, Glover was Black. Again, the officer who shot him was white.

The incident began in the early morning hours of April 28, 1973. Glover and his stepfather were on their way to work. Two undercover officers—in plain clothes, not wearing uniforms—stopped them for questioning in connection with a nearby robbery. Glover and his father turned and ran, believing they were about to be robbed. Glover was shot at least twice. The officer who killed him claimed he had been carrying a weapon, although no weapon was ever located.

Residents of the South Jamaica neighborhood of Queens

---

[68] Jim Dwyer, "A Police Shot to a Boy's Back in Queens, Echoing Since 1973," The *New York Times* (April 16, 2015), https://www.nytimes.com/2015/04/17/nyregion/fired-at-queens-boy-fatal-1973-police-shot-still-reverberates.html.

responded with rioting. Twenty-four people, most of them police officers, were hurt. Twenty-five people were arrested.

A mostly white jury acquitted Thomas Shea, the officer who shot and killed Glover, in 1974. Notably, Shea was the first New York City police officer to be tried for a murder committed while in the course of performing his professional duties.

Houston, TX, Riots, 1978 [69]

Jose Campos Torres, a twenty-three-year-old Mexican-American man and a Vietnam veteran, was arrested in Houston in May 1977. Supposedly he had been involved in a bar fight. When he was presented for booking at the jail, however, the arresting officers' supervisor took one look at him and instructed the officers to transport him to the hospital for treatment. Instead, three days later, Torres' body was found floating in a creek just outside downtown Houston.

Two of the officers who had arrested Torres—Terry W. Denson and Stephen Orlando—were charged with murder. Three other officers were fired but not charged with any crimes. A rookie officer who had been an eyewitness to Torres' torture and then drowning at the hands of Denson and Orlando was the state's star witness. His testimony helped to establish that Torres had been taken to a secluded area in a warehouse district, badly beaten, then dumped into the creek and left to drown.

Denson and Orlando were convicted of a misdemeanor charge of negligent homicide, sentenced to one year of probation, and fined one dollar each. The community exploded. On

---

[69] "Looking back at Houston's Moody Park riot of 1978," https://abc13.com/houstons-moody-park-riot-1978-houston-joe-campos-torres/1326991/.

the one-year anniversary of Torres' death, residents gathered in Moody Park and began chanting "Viva Joe Torres!" and other slogans. Some threw bottles at police officers who had been ordered to clear the area. The rioting spread to nearby businesses. A number of shops were set on fire and looted. One officer was injured when a car ran over him. Two journalists, the first to arrive at the scene, were severely beaten and stabbed.

San Francisco, CA, Riots, 1979 [70]

In the late nineteen seventies, San Francisco was one of the centers of the gay rights movement in the United States, and Harvey Milk was one of its most prominent figures. He was one of the first openly gay men elected to public office, winning a seat on the city's Board of Supervisors in 1977.

Milk and San Francisco Mayor George Moscone were murdered in 1978 by Dan White, a former member of the Board of Supervisors. White was also a former police officer and a former firefighter, and he resigned from his elected position because he claimed he could not make ends meet on his salary. In truth, White had also been running a business that had failed. He changed his mind and attempted to reverse his resignation a few days later, in part due to pressure from his political supporters, many of whom were allied with police and firefighters. When he was not permitted to retake his seat on the Board, he snuck into the city hall, eluding metal detectors, and shot and killed Moscone and Milk.

Prosecutors charged White with first-degree murder and alleged the existence of special circumstances which, if found,

---

[70] Martin Stezano, "What Were the White Night Riots?" History.com (Jun 7, 2017), https://www.history.com/news/what-were-the-white-night-riots.

would permit imposition of the death penalty. However, White and his defense team asserted a controversial defense, since nicknamed the "Twinkie" defense, in which he claimed that he could not have formed the necessary intent to commit murder because he had been gorging on junk food around the time of the crime. In reality, what he claimed was more akin to severe depression. Several of White's friends and associates with the police department testified that it was common for politicians to be carrying weapons at that time and also that people often entered city hall through a window, supposedly to save time. However these allegations might sound now, they were accepted by the jury, and White was convicted only of voluntary manslaughter.

The trial played out against a backdrop that had involved many years of police harassment of gay men and gay men's clubs. The Stonewall Riots had taken place around ten years before on the East Coast, and the White Night Riots in San Francisco were to be the West Coast's counterpart. Dan White came to stand for the city's conservative communities, and, in particular, he was associated with the law enforcement officers who had been harassing residents of the Castro for years. Around 1500 outraged people gathered and began to march along Castro Street. As with other riots, marchers damaged and set fire to police cars and other property. One of them shouted to onlookers that, if arrested, he would allege the Twinkie defense.

White committed suicide in 1985 after serving only five years of his seven-year sentence. According to the officer who had arrested him in 1978, White eventually confessed that the killings had, in fact, been premeditated. He allegedly had also planned to kill two other politicians at the time.

Miami Riots, 1980 [71]

Violent responses to perceived injustice continued in 1980. In the spring of that year, four Dade County Safety Department officers were acquitted in the beating death of Arthur McDuffie. McDuffie was a thirty-three-year-old Black man, an insurance salesman and former Marine who, according to police, failed to stop for a stop sign on December 17, 1979. Six white police officers gave chase. McDuffie was driving a motorcycle, but his license had been suspended for traffic violations. The officers claimed that McDuffie lost control of his motorcycle and was thrown to the ground, striking his head. They admitted that he was then surrounded and beaten, supposedly because he had attempted to kick one of the officers. The evidence later established that the officers drove a police cruiser over McDuffie's motorcycle to simulate a traffic accident.

McDuffie died at a hospital four days after the arrest. He had sustained multiple skull fractures, and his injuries were not consistent with a fall from a motorcycle. Instead, the arresting officer had pulled McDuffie from his motorcycle and then, with the assistance of other officers who arrived shortly thereafter, had beaten him to death with nightsticks and police-issue flashlights. These blows were landed after McDuffie had been handcuffed and subdued. Officers also used a tire iron to mark the asphalt to simulate skid marks and removed McDuffie's watch and threw it in a ditch. Not only was McDuffie the victim of a police beating, but he was also the victim of an elaborate cover-up. The officers were charged with various crimes ranging from manslaughter to tampering with evidence.

---

[71] "Miami riots 1980: My friend was killed by my colleagues," BBC News (May 21, 2020), https://www.bbc.com/news/av/stories-52736475.

The trial was moved from Miami to Tampa due to simmering tensions around the killing and because of pretrial publicity. Janet Reno, who would later be appointed Attorney General under President William Clinton, prosecuted the case. The court granted a directed verdict in favor of one of the officers, meaning that the judge ruled as a matter of law that the charges against him had not been proved. A jury acquitted the rest of the defendants. One juror told the press he believed McDuffie's death was tragic but that the state had rushed the case to trial.

Something like 5000 people filled the streets outside the courthouse after the verdicts were announced. Protestors, in some cases, turned on innocent civilians. Three white men driving home from a fishing trip were dragged from their car and beaten to death. Another man was ambushed on his way from work. In his desperate attempt to escape stones being thrown at his car, he crashed into a wall. Thus trapped, he burned to death when his car was set alight. Property damage was in the range of $100 million.

Miami Riots, 1989 [72]

Miami was plagued by yet more unrest only nine years later. The police officer on this occasion, William Lozano, shot a man, Clement Lloyd, who was fleeing from officers on a motorcycle. Lloyd was fatally shot in the head and crashed into another vehicle, killing his passenger, Allan Blanchard. Lozano alleged that Lloyd tried to run him over and, therefore, the shooting was in self-defense. Rioting broke out immediately

---

[72] Jeffrey Schmalz, "Miami Officer Guilty in 2 Killings That Prompted Rioting by Blacks," The *New York Times* (Dec. 8, 1989), https://www.nytimes.com/1989/12/08/us/miami-officer-guilty-in-2-killings-that-prompted-rioting-by-blacks.html.

after the shooting and lasted for several days.

Lozano was tried for manslaughter in the deaths of the two Black men, and he was initially convicted. However, he was granted a new trial on appeal because the appeals court found that the pretrial riots had likely prejudiced the jury. Jurors were afraid that if they announced a not-guilty verdict, more violence would follow:

> *"We simply cannot approve the result of a trial conducted, as was this one, in an atmosphere in which the entire community, including the jury, was so obviously ... so justifiably concerned with the dangers which would follow an acquittal."*

Additionally, the prosecutor had been allowed to introduce evidence concerning police procedures and training that the court found inadmissible. When Lozano was retried, he was acquitted.

Los Angeles Riots, 1992 [73]

The Los Angeles, CA riots of 1992 are among the most famous such incidents in recent years, in part because they were covered extensively by new national cable television channels such as CNN. They arose from yet another police-involved beating. The victim was Rodney King. During the evening of March 3, 1991, police officers attempted to pull over King, who was traveling at a high speed with two passengers in his car. Once the chase ended, King was quickly surrounded by five LAPD officers who tasered him, tackled him, hit him with their batons, and kicked and stomped on his prone body.

---

[73] Lou Cannon. *Official Negligence: How Rodney King and the Riots Changed Los Angeles and the LAPD.* Basic Books (2002).

Sergeant Stacey Koon claimed that he believed King was resisting arrest and was under the influence of PCP at the time of his arrest. The arrest, however, had been caught on film by a private citizen standing on a nearby balcony. The footage showed that King made an initial, aborted effort to escape but had been quickly brought to the ground and then beaten by officers with little resistance on his part. The public was, for one of the first times, able to see police brutality in action, and they were outraged.

Testing later proved that there was no PCP in King's system when he was arrested.

Police Chief Darryl Gates was shocked by the film:

I stared at the screen in disbelief. I played the one-minute-fifty-second tape again. Then again and again, until I had viewed it 25 times. And still I could not believe what I was looking at. To see my officers engage in what appeared to be excessive use of force, possibly criminally excessive, to see them beat a man with their batons 56 times, to see a sergeant on the scene who did nothing to seize control, was something I never dreamed I would witness.[74]

The district attorney charged four of the officers with assault and use of excessive force. Media coverage was intense, and to ensure a fair trial, the proceedings were moved to Ventura County, a far more rural and wealthy area of California. The jury acquitted three officers on April 29, 1992. They were unable to reach a verdict with respect to the fourth officer.

Many were incredulous. The video footage of the beatings seemed self-explanatory. Los Angeles Mayor Tom Bradley—

---

[74] Lou Cannon, "In Book, Gates Confesses To A 'Significant Error,'" The *Washington Post* (May 19, 1992), https://www.washingtonpost.com/archive/politics/1992/05/19/in-book-gates-confesses-to-a-significant-error/5b3b664c-4d0d-430a-963e-8f5753c4d4b3/.

only the second Black man elected to lead a major American city—said, immediately following the verdict:

> "Today, this jury told the world that what we all saw with our own eyes wasn't a crime. Today, that jury asked us to accept the senseless and brutal beating of a helpless man. Today, that jury said we should tolerate such conduct by those sworn to protect and serve. My friends, I am here to tell this jury, 'No. No, our eyes did not deceive us. We saw what we saw... what we saw was a crime...' We must not endanger the reforms we have achieved by resorting to mindless acts. We must not push back progress by striking back blindly."

Some have suggested that Mayor Bradley's remarks inspired or tacitly permitted the rioting that followed the verdict.[75] Violence intensified over the days that followed. Sixty-four people died, ten of whom were shot by law enforcement officers. Property losses ranged between $800 million and $1 billion, a staggering sum. More than 1,000 buildings were set on fire and destroyed. Looting was widespread, again, in many cases, caught on television cameras and broadcasted to the country. Interracial conflict motivated some of the property-directed violence, as many in the Black community had felt for some time that Korean shopkeepers were discriminating against them.

In another famously televised incident, a group of Black men pulled white truck driver Reginald Denny from his vehicle and beat him severely. One of the attackers executed a football-style victory dance at the conclusion of the attack.

Many commentators blame Gates for the severity of the

---

[75] April Wolfe, "10 Things we learned about the L.A. Riots from L.A. 92," *LA Weekly* (Apr. 20, 2017), https://www.laweekly.com/10-things-we-learned-about-the-l-a-riots-from-la-92/.

1992 riots. During the time he served as chief of the department, incidents of employment racial harassment as well as claims of racially motivated police brutality soared. Gates adopted the Broken Windows style of policing when he joined the department and, for many years, enforced Operation Hammer, a program under which Black and Hispanic young men were targeted for arrest.

Cincinnati Riots, 2001 [76]

The city of Cincinnati was visited by civil unrest in 2001 after three men were killed in police custody in unrelated incidents. The first man, Roger Owensby, Jr., was asphyxiated while being held in a chokehold on November 7, 2000. Jeffrey Irons died the following day after a fight with police officers. Five months later, yet another man, Timothy Thomas, was shot and killed in a confrontation with officers trying to arrest him on multiple bench warrants. The officer, Patrolman Stephen Roach, claimed that Thomas was reaching for a gun. An investigation later established that he had only been pulling up his pants.

Protestors collected outside the city government building while the city council was in session and issued a call for explanations. They were told only that the investigation was ongoing. Meanwhile, the city council members holed up in the building, refusing to face the crowd of people waiting outside. Protestors began throwing stones and other items at a line of officers standing between them and the building. Officers fired tear gas, bean bags, and rubber bullets back at the protestors. Unsatisfied with the government's response to their demand

---

[76] David Childs and Ryan Spence, "The Cincinnati Race Riots of 2001," *Oxford University Press* (May 31, 2018), https://doi.org/10.1093/acref/9780 195301731.013.78142.

for information, protestors eventually made their way downtown, destroying property along the way. Sixty-six of them were arrested.

All three of the officers stood trial, and none of them was convicted of any crime. Two of them were acquitted outright. One defendant's trial ended in a hung jury, and charges were not refiled.

Oakland Riots, 2010 [77]

The Cincinnati riots were just the beginning of civil unrest stemming from the public's demand for justice in the first years of the new millennium. On January 1, 2009, Bay Area Rapid Transit (BART) police officers were summoned to a train with reports of a fight between passengers. Officer Anthony Pirone subdued Oscar Grant, forcing him to lie face down on the train platform. Pirone's partner, Johannes Mehserle, then drew his weapon and shot Grant in the back. The killing was, as in the King case, filmed, this time by multiple bystanders as well as stationary surveillance cameras. Police allegedly tried to confiscate witnesses' cell phones after the shooting. Grant was rushed to the hospital and died.

Mehserle resigned his position when he was charged with second-degree murder. He claimed that he had shot Grant accidentally because he believed he was aiming his Taser, not his service weapon, at the man. Expert witnesses offered contradicting opinions, with one saying that he believed the killing had amounted to an execution and another saying he believed the shooting was accidental. Mehserle had quickly "lawyered

---

[77] "78 protesters arrested after verdict in killing of unarmed black man," CNN.com (July 9, 2010), http://www.cnn.com/2010/CRIME/07/08/subway.shooting.trial.riot/index.html.

up" after the incident, and he refused to cooperate with the police investigation or to speak with the press, a move that itself contributed to rising anger and frustration. Before taking on the case, Mehserle's attorney had made statements that juries generally believe police officers when shootings occur. In fact, a jury accepted Mehserle's explanation for the incident. They returned a verdict of guilty on the charge of involuntary manslaughter and acquitted him on the more serious charges of murder and voluntary manslaughter.

A report prepared by internal affairs, the BART division responsible for investigating the conduct of police officers, indicated that Mehserle lied about confusing his Taser with his sidearm. Additionally, BART determined that Mehserle was "responsible for setting the events in motion that created a chaotic and tense situation on the platform, setting the stage, even if inadvertent, for the shooting of Oscar Grant."[78] The report was not made available to the jury who decided the criminal case, however.

The protests that followed the announcement of the verdict in July 2010 were, for the most part, peaceful. Looting, arson, and property destruction occurred on a sporadic basis after dark. Around eighty people were eventually arrested in connection with riots and protests.

New York City Riots, 2014

In 2014, another Black citizen lost his life in the course of an arrest. This incident was again filmed, and the release of the

---

[78] Dakin Andone and Marlena Baldacci, "Officer instigated then lied about actions that led to shooting death of Oscar Grant, report says," CNN.com (May 4, 2019), https://www.cnn.com/2019/05/04/us/oscar-grant-shooting-bart-internal-investigation/index.html.

film led to widespread protests. People seeking greater police accountability have since adopted Eric Garner's plea for help—"I can't breathe"—as a slogan and mantra.[79]

Garner died because he allegedly sold cigarettes illegally. In New York City, cigarettes are taxed, and packs of cigarettes must carry a stamp. Garner sold single cigarettes on the street, which was a misdemeanor. When police officers approached him on July 17, 2014, he complained that they continually harassed him and that he was tired of cooperating with them. In other words, Garner had been the target of frequent Broken Windows-style stops, and he voiced his frustration with the approach.

Officer Daniel Pantaleo responded by placing his hands on Garner, who pulled away. Pantaleo considered this an effort to resist arrest, justifying additional force. He wrestled Garner to the ground and placed him in a chokehold. Additional police officers applied their weight to Garner's body, pinning him down. Garner stated, "I can't breathe," eleven times while he lay face down on the sidewalk. Then he lost consciousness.

Pantaleo and the other police officers allowed Garner to remain on the sidewalk for seven minutes while they waited for an ambulance to arrive. He was pronounced dead roughly one hour later. The Office of the Medical Examiner for New York City concluded that Garner had died by homicide, meaning that the police officers effecting his arrest had intentionally caused his death by compressing his neck and chest. A cell phone video of the arrest, taken by a member of Copwatch, an activist group, circulated on news and social media.[80] A grand

---

[79] Nicholas St. Fleur, "They Shouted 'I Can't Breathe,'" The *Atlantic* (Dec. 4, 2014), https://www.theatlantic.com/national/archive/2014/12/New-York-City-Eric-Garner-Protests/383415/.

[80] That activist, Ramsey Orta, claims that he was harassed after releasing the film to the public, and says that law enforcement went so far as to poison his and other prisoners' food while he was being held at Rikers

jury refused to indict Pantaleo on December 4, 2014. The public reacted with protests and rallies, not only locally but nationwide. An internal disciplinary proceeding against Pantaleo followed. He was finally terminated in August 2019, five years after Garner died. An indictment was sought a second time, and again the grand jury declined. Garner's family filed a civil suit against the City of New York, which was settled for nearly $6 million.

The Missouri Riots, 2014 [81]

The country had little time to catch its breath after Eric Garner's death. The death of Michael Brown a few months later perhaps initiated a new era in the public's reaction to police-involved shootings, although the facts of the case were sadly similar to those in so many others. The groundwork was laid on August 9, 2014, when Brown and an acquaintance, Doran Johnson, were simply walking on a street in Ferguson, Missouri. Officer Darren Wilson demanded that Brown and Johnson move from the street to the sidewalk, and then he stopped his police vehicle in front of them in order to confront them. He and Brown had an altercation through the open window of the police car, during which Wilson fired twice. Brown and Johnson ran, and Wilson exited his car to pursue them. At some point, Brown turned to face Wilson, who then fired

Island on weapons charges. Lab tests conducted at the request of a lawyer for the prisoners confirmed the presence of brodifacoum, rat poison, in the food. Emma Whitford, "Lab Tests Confirm That Rikers Meatloaf Had Rat Poison," Gothamist, https://gothamist.com/news/lab-tests-confirm-that-rikers-meatloaf-had-rat-poison.

[81] "What happened in Ferguson?" The *New York Times* (Aug. 10, 2015), https://www.nytimes.com/interactive/2014/08/13/us/ferguson-missouri-town-under-siege-after-police-shooting.html.

twelve shots, six of which hit Brown.

Wilson alleged that Brown attacked him inside his police vehicle and tried to take control of his service weapon. Johnson disputed that account. He said that Wilson grabbed Brown by the neck through the patrol car window, threatened him, and then shot at him. Wilson and Johnson agreed that Brown and Johnson fled, with Wilson pursuing Brown shortly thereafter. Wilson claimed that he fired in self-defense as Brown charged at him, which Johnson denied. A witness claimed that Wilson warned Brown he would open fire and that Brown cried out, "Don't shoot!" before he was killed.

As the details of the shooting emerged, Ferguson police established curfews and deployed riot squads to maintain order. The city descended into unrest, with looting and occasional violence. The media arrived quickly and began reporting from the scene. News reports depicted a heavily militarized police force deployed to face off against protestors. If law enforcement was feeling the consequences of the breakdown of its relations with the Black community, it responded not with attempts at communication and understanding but with armored vehicles and tear gas.[82]

---

[82] Many policy discussions in the aftermath of Brown's death focused on the level of force and military-style weaponry utilized by local police in response to demonstrations. To begin with, law enforcement agencies seemed to be operating from the assumption that such protests were improper or illegal when in fact civil disobedience, as distinguished from violent rioting, is a Constitutionally protected activity. In some cases, this attitude served to egg on violence by establishing an "us versus them" mentality on both sides. That circumstance was only worsened by officers' donning highly militarized gear, carrying assault weapons, and travelling in armored vehicles more like tanks than cars. This problem has attracted attention from both liberal and conservative members of Congress and led to calls for changes to a law that, since the 1990s, has supplied local police forces with surplus military equipment.

The Department of Defense initiative, known as the "1033 program,"

The unrest continued into November when a grand jury elected not to indict Wilson. The DOJ likewise concluded that Wilson had shot Brown in self-defense and declined to seek its own charges against him. Nevertheless, the DOJ also conducted an investigation into Ferguson's policing practices and announced that the Ferguson Police Department had engaged in misconduct. This included discrimination against African-American people and utilizing racial stereotypes in a "pattern or practice of unlawful conduct."[83] Many refer to this practice as "profiling."

The deaths of Michael Brown and Eric Garner spotlighted an issue that had not been widely discussed previously: the use of grand juries in police-involved shooting investigations. Prosecutors can generally initiate criminal cases by two methods. They can file charges against a defendant or they can seek an indictment by way of a grand jury. Grand juries hear evidence submitted to them by prosecutors. If the grand jury decides that the evidence is sufficient, it issues an indictment.

This means that the prosecution is in full control of the evidence. Criminal defense attorneys often complain that grand juries don't hear the full story since they don't hear evidence from the defendant's witnesses. It is, however, also true that a prosecutor who would prefer that an indictment not be issued can decide against putting all of the available evidence

---

was developed to support law enforcement personnel in the fight against drug gangs, many of whom were heavily armed. The people of Ferguson and others who participated in protests against police violence in the ensuing years were, of course, not associated with heavily armed drug cartels. "Despite Current Debate, Police Militarization Goes Beyond U.S. Borders," Inter Press Service (ipsnews.net), http://www.ipsnews.net/2014/08/despite-current-debate-police-militarisation-goes-beyond-u-s-borders/.

[83] Investigation of the Ferguson Police Department: United States Department of Justice Civil Rights Division, https://www.justice.gov/sites/default/files/opa/press-releases/attachments/2015/03/04/ferguson_police_department_report.pdf.

before the grand jury.[84] District attorneys are law enforcement officers, and they work closely with police officers. Prosecutors depend on officers to arrest criminals and assemble the evidence necessary to convict. That relationship has proved thorny when the suspect or defendant is a police officer.

Historically, grand juries acted more independently. Rather than passively receiving and considering the state's evidence, grand juries were empowered to issue their own subpoenas and steer their own investigations. This was, in and of itself, a very powerful check on governmental power. The grand juries that decided against indicting Darren Wilson and Daniel Pantaleo relied on the evidence they received from prosecutors. Many have charged that this process was tainted. Many believe that the failure to obtain charges against Pantaleo and Wilson was not indicative at all of a just system.

Baltimore Riots: 2015 [85]

Freddie Gray died in Baltimore police custody months later. The facts and circumstances of his arrest and death, as well as the riots that followed, have already been summarized. Of the officers who were involved, two were white. Four were Black.

Baltimore's State's Attorney in 2015 was a Black woman, Marilyn Mosby. On May 1, 2015, after a press conference in

---

[84] "Grand Jury - Should The Grand Jury Be Abolished? - Critics, Prosecutor, Juries, and Criminal," JRank Articles, https://law.jrank.org/pages/7197/Grand-Jury-SHOULD-GRAND-JURY-BE-ABOLISHED.html.

[85] "Freddie Gray: The death that shook the city of Baltimore," The *Baltimore Sun* (Dec. 27, 2015), https://www.baltimoresun.com/maryland/bs-md-yir-freddie-gray-20151224-story.html?gclid=Cj0KCQiAjJOQBhCkARIs AEKMtO3MS0sCdbYIrINugOo-PxUN719Chatm5G9nAQZl_WaLnC5Ll0R8f llaAs4HEALw_wcB.

which she stated that she had heard the protestors' chants of "no justice, no peace," Mosby filed charges against six of the officers involved in Gray's arrest and transport. The officer who had driven the van with Gray unsecured inside it received the most serious charge for second-degree "depraved heart" murder. A person who commits a "depraved heart" killing has shown callous disregard for human life. Other officers were charged with lesser crimes, ranging in seriousness from manslaughter to illegal arrest. A grand jury issued an indictment on the charges a few weeks later.

The decision was made to try each police officer separately.[86] From the outset, prosecutors found themselves at odds with Judge Barry Williams of the Baltimore City Circuit Court, who had a very different view of the evidence in the case. Judge Williams believed that prosecutors were holding the officers responsible for failing to comply with safety rules that they had not been made aware of. He also believed that there was insufficient evidence that the officers knew they were putting Gray at substantial risk of harm or that they knowingly disregarded that risk. One of the charges filed, reckless endangerment, could not be proved because the reckless endangerment statute specifically excluded conduct committed while using a motor vehicle.

The jury in the case against Officer William Porter, who was called to check on Gray and found him unconscious in the back of the van, ended in a mistrial. Officers Edward Nero, Caesar Goodman, and Brian Rice elected bench trials, meaning that a judge heard their cases and rendered verdicts instead of submitting the cases to juries. Each of them, including Goodson, the driver of the van, was acquitted. Charges against the

---

[86] Amelia McDonell-Parry & Justine Barron, "Death of Freddie Gray: 5 Things You Didn't Know," *Rolling Stone* (Apr. 12, 2017), https://www.rollingstone.com/culture/culture-features/death-of-freddie-gray-5-things-you-didnt-know-129327/.

remaining defendants were dropped in July 2016. Commentators have generally considered the trials a failure on Mosby's part, with some pointing out that Mosby was both an inexperienced trial attorney and politician at the time of Gray's death. In 2022, she was defeated in a primary election.

The Baltimore Police Department has remained embroiled in controversy. In 2017, eight members of its Gun Trace Task Force were charged with racketeering crimes. Crime rates in the city have soared. While the allegation is unproven, it has been suggested that a breakdown in trust between Mosby's team and the Department, coupled with increased oversight of the Department after Gray's death, resulted in an overall slowdown of police work.[87]

Nationwide Protests & Riots: 2020

The year 2020 will be remembered for many reasons. It was the year of a widespread pandemic that left no country unscathed. By the end of 2020, more than a million people around the world had died as a result of COVID-19. But while the pandemic raged, the United States saw widespread protests and riots sparked by yet another police-involved death. A Black Minneapolis man by the name of George Floyd had pleaded for his life as he lay on the ground, unable to breathe for more than nine minutes while a police officer knelt on Floyd's neck. Floyd died in front of multiple witnesses—one of whom recorded the entire scene on her phone. Like Eric Garner, Floyd was asphyxiated to death.

The recording of Garner's arrest and death was widely shared on social media in 2014. The recording of Floyd's death

---

[87] Alec MacGillis, "What Can Mayors Do When The Police Stop Doing Their Jobs," *ProPublica* (Sept. 20, 2020), https://www.propublica.org/article/what-can-mayors-do-when-the-police-stop-doing-their-jobs.

similarly was posted to Facebook, Twitter, Instagram, and TikTok accounts around the world, with one significant difference: people were home. With schools and businesses shut down because of the pandemic, people had little else to do but watch television and search the web. Coals that had been glowing for years after the deaths of James Powell, Martin Chambers, Michael Brown, and others burst into flame. The evidence of Floyd's abuse at the hands of law enforcement officers seemed incontrovertible.

The Black Lives Matter movement brought people from all walks of life together to promote a common cause. "I can't breathe" became the mantra of protests that, at times, turned violent.

The events that would end Floyd's life began on May 25, 2020. Floyd visited a local bodega to purchase cigarettes. He was a frequent and good customer, but on this day, the owner was not in, and the store clerk who was working did not recognize Floyd. The clerk accused Floyd of paying with a counterfeit bill and demanded that he hand back the pack of cigarettes he had just purchased. Floyd refused. The police were summoned.

When they reached the scene, Floyd was sitting in a car with two other passengers. One officer approached, gun drawn, and dragged Floyd from the vehicle. That officer claimed that Floyd resisted being handcuffed, although, of course, that seems understandable—Floyd had done nothing wrong. Once he had been handcuffed, Floyd was cooperative. When officers attempted to place him in the back of a patrol car, however, Floyd resisted and fell to the ground. He told officers he was claustrophobic.

At this time, several other officers, including Derek Chauvin, arrived to assist in the arrest. Chauvin pulled Floyd away from the vehicle and allowed him to fall to the ground. Then, as Floyd lay prone, handcuffed, facing the ground,

Chauvin placed his knee on Floyd's neck and kept it there for nine full minutes. Two other officers pressed on Chauvin's back. Whatever officers might have claimed led to other arrest-related deaths, there was simply no reasonable basis for this treatment of a man who had demonstrated no violence, no serious resistance, and no hostility.

The officers were wearing body cameras, and the cameras captured the arrest. Floyd could be heard pleading for his life. He stated that he was unable to breathe more than twenty times. At one point, he said, "You're going to kill me, man." Chauvin told him to stop wasting oxygen by talking. Floyd asked onlookers to tell his mother and his children that he loved them and became unresponsive.

One of the officers checked for a pulse and could not find one. No other assistance was offered. The officers who had choked a man to death stood by and did nothing. When an ambulance finally arrived, it transported Floyd to a hospital, where he was pronounced dead.

Protests began within twenty-four hours, both across the United States and in many other countries. Some of these protests turned violent. The spring of 2020 would become the most destructive period of unrest in the United States after the 1992 riots in Los Angeles, with two people killed, 604 people arrested, and property damage exceeding $2 billion.[88] Of course, it is impossible to quantify the damage done in human terms. One of Floyd's friends, Christopher Harris, called Floyd's death "senseless." Additionally:

"He begged for his life. He pleaded for his life. When you try so hard to put faith in this system, a system that you know

---

[88] Brad Polumbo, "George Floyd Riots Caused Record-Setting $2 Billion in Damage, New Report Says. Here's Why the True Cost Is Even Higher," Fee.org (Sept. 16, 2020), https://fee.org/articles/george-floyd-riots-caused-record-setting-2-billion-in-damage-new-report-says-here-s-why-the-true-cost-is-even-higher/.

isn't designed for you, when you constantly seek justice by lawful means and you can't get it, you begin to take the law into your own hands."

Chauvin was convicted in 2021 of second-degree unintentional murder, third-degree murder, and second-degree manslaughter for killing Floyd. The former Minneapolis Police officer was sentenced to twenty-two and a half years in prison. He eventually pled guilty to federal charges brought against him.[89]

The Floyd family praised these results while acknowledging the troubling truth of police brutality, for which officers have generally not been held responsible:

> *For once, a police officer who wrongly took the life of a Black man was held to account. While this shouldn't be exceptional, tragically it is. Day after day, year after year, police kill Black people without consequence. But today, with Chauvin's sentence, we take a significant step forward—something that was unimaginable a very short time ago.*[90]

According to a survey by National Public Radio, police officers have shot and killed at least 135 unarmed Black men and women since 2015. In those instances, at least seventy-five percent of the officers were white. Only a few such officers were indicted in connection with the shootings, and even fewer were convicted.[91]

---

[89] Bill Chappell, "Derek Chauvin Is Sentenced to 22 ½ Years for George Floyd's Murder," NPR (June 25, 2021), https://www.npr.org/sections/trial-over-killing-of-george-floyd/.

[90] Emma Bowman, "Minneapolis Reacts To Chauvin Sentence With Fury And Hope," NPR (June 25, 2021), https://www.npr.org/sections/trial-over-killing-of-george-floyd/.

[91] *Id.*

Police officers are uniquely situated because, by virtue of their jobs, they have unusual power and authority. When they abuse their power, they have the potential to cause extraordinary damage. According to "The History of Police Brutality," an article published by the National Trial Lawyers Association in 2020:

> *Most police officers are committed and ethical. They work a difficult, life-threatening job, and their days are extraordinarily stressful. However, police officers also exercise a great deal of control over the lives of the people they interact with, and an abuse of this power is particularly egregious. The physical, emotional, financial, and legal consequences of police brutality can be staggering.*[92]

---

[92] The History of American Police Brutality," The National Trial Lawyers Association (June 27, 2020), https://thenationaltriallawyers.org/2020/07/the-history-of-american-police-brutality/.

CHAPTER ELEVEN

Lack of Resources and Inconsistent Outcomes

"Do the best you can, no matter how unimportant it may seem at the time. No one learns more about a problem than the person at the bottom." [93]

WAS OUR SYSTEM ESTABLISHED for a smaller population that has since grown to exceed the system's capacity? Was it designed for a time when there was less crime per capita than there is today?

There are thousands of local jurisdictions across the United States, and each of them is charged with administering its own criminal justice system and laws. In addition, the federal government is authorized to prosecute federal criminal laws for certain offenses committed within the states, adding additional complexity to a system that has become positively baroque.

Despite the multiple layers of laws and law enforcement in any given jurisdiction, the district and state's attorneys are expected to ensure that laws are enforced uniformly. This task

---

[93] Justice Sandra Day O'Connor (1981–2006).

is virtually impossible given differences in populations, crime rates, resources, and other practicalities. Every jurisdiction is required to provide a speedy trial to those who are accused of crimes, for example, but not every jurisdiction has the money and personnel necessary to actually do that.

The State's Attorney's Office for Baltimore City, like many such offices across the country, is consistently starved for resources. For that reason, even though the city is affected by significantly more crimes than in surrounding jurisdictions, prosecutors must allocate available resources. That means making difficult choices about which crimes are prosecuted.

This means that serious criminals are sometimes allowed to slip through the cracks. One awful episode in Baltimore's history brought this reality into sharp focus. Angela Dawson, her husband, and five children were callously murdered in a firebombing on October 17, 2002. The fire—one of the worst arsons in the city's history—was set in retaliation for Dawson's repeated complaints to police about neighborhood drug dealers.

Darrell Brooks pled guilty to the crime in federal court and is serving a life sentence without parole. During the pre-trial proceedings, the City of Baltimore conceded that Brooks could have been jailed months before the murders because he had failed to report to his probation agent. Brooks was on probation when he kicked open the Dawson's kitchen door in the early morning hours, splashed gasoline onto the floor, and then set it on fire. The fire killed Angela Maria Dawson, 36, and her five children: Keith Dawson, 9; Kevin Dawson, 9; Carnell Dawson, Jr., 10; Juan Ortiz, 12; and LaWanda Ortiz, 14. Angela Dawson's husband, Carnell Dawson Sr., 43, died from head injuries he sustained trying to escape the fire.

"To date, we have not found any documented contact (with a probation agent) and that is reprehensible," said Stuart O. Simms, Secretary of the Department of Public Safety and

Correctional Services.[94] Brooks had been on two years' probation following a three-year suspended sentence for unauthorized use of a motor vehicle. Six other charges, including theft and drug possession, were dropped. One of the goals of probation as a tool in the criminal justice system is to allow offenders to remain in or return to the community with oversight. But Brooks never had any contact with his probation agent, meaning that he had no oversight. And Brooks' probation agent never reported his failure to be in contact, Simms noted.

Brooks had a long history of run-ins with city police. He committed or was charged with committing a string of armed robberies, assaults, and other offenses dating back at least to 1998. How could the community be anything but angry? Angela Dawson had tried to be a good citizen. She called the police to complain about drug dealing in her neighborhood, hoping that the neighborhood would be made safe. Instead, she and her family were murdered for "snitching."

The War Room

Officials relied on Darrell Brooks' case to push through an initiative they named the "War Room"—a multi-agency criminal justice task force that would share information to identify and track violent repeat offenders. A staff of attorneys, law clerks, IT specialists, and parole and probation employees manned the War Room eighteen hours a day. Their primary targets were career criminals already on parole or probation for violent crimes or gun offenses. The team also flagged weapons or violent crime offenders who were arrested while they were

---

[94] Laurie Wills, "Suspect in fire skirted probation," The *Baltimore Sun* (Oct. 19, 2002), https://www.baltimoresun.com/news/bs-xpm-2002-10-19-02 10190315-story.html.

already on parole or probation for any offense or while they had other charges pending.

Then there were the "predetermineds"—a watch list compiled by a multi-agency working group composed of the Baltimore City State's Attorney's Office, the Washington-Baltimore High Intensity Drug Trafficking Area, the Bureau of Alcohol, Tobacco and Firearms, the U.S. Attorney's Office, the Baltimore City Police Department, and state and federal parole and probation agencies.

Once a War Room offender was identified, the Baltimore City State's Attorney's Office would press judges to decide whether to revoke the offender's parole or probation. As a prosecutor, I would frequently be given a file stamped "WR" for "War Room." We were instructed by the State's Attorney to take the case to trial or, in negotiating a plea bargain, to not accept anything less than the office's minimum sentence for such an offender and offense. We were told to avoid dismissing the case at all costs.

Targets were identified and surveilled. If they committed even low-level offenses, the police would bring them in. Spitting, jaywalking, it did not matter; the mantra was to harass these offenders until they either went to prison or moved somewhere else to live.

Before becoming a prosecutor, back when I was a law student, the Baltimore City Police Department regularly visited us in the briefing room for the clinical law program at the University of Maryland School of Law. They assured us that they knew who the bad guys were and that they were going to do everything they could to make the bad guys' lives a living hell. Either they would leave Baltimore, or they would head to prison. They watched these individuals all day, every day, waiting for them to make a mistake. If any violation of the law occurred, an officer was standing by to conduct a stop-and-frisk; quite often, this search turned up contraband justifying more serious charges.

This approach was theoretically a good one. It narrowed the field of potential criminals to those who were deemed truly dangerous. But even this smaller net remained large enough to allow for many stop-and-frisks or traffic stops on law-abiding citizens who satisfied no other criterion than that they were Black and lived in a Black neighborhood.

An Overwhelming Caseload

The criminal conviction rate is inherently proportional to the number of judges and jurors available each day to hear criminal trials and proceedings. There are realistically only so many seats for jurors to fill in a courthouse and only so many citizens a day who can afford to step away from work and family to serve. A jurisdiction with 300 criminal cases on its docket for a given day will struggle much more to resolve its cases than a jurisdiction with only twenty cases on the docket. More densely populated areas will have more crimes; however, urban areas have *much higher* rates of crime per capita than most suburban or rural areas. The constitutionally guaranteed rights to counsel and speedy trial, however, apply to all defendants, whether they are being tried in a busy court system or not. Courts on the eastern shore of Maryland simply do not have to manage the administrative burdens that plague the Circuit Court for Baltimore City.

For example, Kent County, which is located just across the Chesapeake Bay Bridge, has a current population of just over 19,000 people and may only have ten criminal cases on its docket each day. Of those cases, many will be non-violent, and many will be resolved via plea bargain without a jury. That's a number the court can handle with 150 jurors each day. Even if every criminal defendant on the docket winds up requesting a jury trial, there will be enough jurors on the panel to accommodate that request. This is not the case in Baltimore City, which has a current population of over 500,000 and averages at least 300 or more cases a day.

The number of cases to be resolved each day also impacts the amount of time defendants who are convicted and incarcerated can expect to serve. Given the numbers above and the chart listed as Exhibit 1, it is easy to understand why more rural jurisdictions can incarcerate their offenders for more time than Baltimore City can. For example, a defendant found guilty of simple drug possession is sentenced in most Maryland counties to serve around sixteen months. In Baltimore City, the same defendant will serve less than two months. There are just too many defendants and too few jury panels and judges available to administrate this volume of cases.

Affording all criminal defendants the right to a jury trial, the right to a speedy trial, the right to representation by counsel, the right to confront witnesses, and the right against self-incrimination taxes the resources of busy jurisdictions such as the City of Baltimore to the point of gridlock. These rights can only be made available by dedicating vast resources to them. The largest such resource is manpower.

Docket Administration in Baltimore, MD

When a defendant first appears for trial in Baltimore City, he or she is advised of his or her right to an attorney. The court must postpone the case to allow the defendant to obtain counsel if he or she is not already represented but wants a lawyer's advice. When the case returns for trial after weeks or months, all of the parties are asked if they are prepared. Sometimes the state's witnesses are unavailable at the time. Another postponement may therefore be granted. Meanwhile, the speedy trial clock is ticking. The court can only grant so many post-ponements before the defendant's right to a speedy trial ac-crues—at which time the case could be dismissed entirely.

By the time the case is ready for trial, given the extremely high volume of crime in Baltimore City, it may be competing for a courtroom with 300 other cases on any given day. Balti-more City generally summons 500 citizens a day to serve as potential jurors. Groups of these potential jurors are brought into the courtroom, and the individual potential jurors are questioned by the attorneys to determine whether they could not serve for any reason in a process known as *voir dire*. Clearly, only a handful of these 300 cases can actually be ac-commodated on a given day. That means the prosecutor must find a way to resolve the vast majority of those cases short of trial. He or she will need to pick the most winnable cases or the cases that involve the most concerning defendants to be tried. The other cases, the ones involving less violent offenses, first offenses, or cases with evidentiary issues, will be plea bar-gained or dismissed. Remember, trials cannot be postponed indefinitely.

With around thirty-five Circuit Court judges in Baltimore City, and as some of those judges must hear other kinds of cases (civil cases, workers' compensation, and other adminis-trative appeals), the system can only handle twenty-five to thirty jury trials in a day. That leaves 275 criminal cases every day that cannot be tried. Around half of them can be post-poned for one reason or another without jeopardizing the case. Almost 140 cases, then, must be resolved in some other way. Every day, 140 criminal defendants either enter into plea bargains (usually agreeing to plead guilty to offenses that are less serious than the ones they were charged with) or they are released altogether (the charges against them dismissed).

The Daily Grind: Case Disposal

Judges often tell defendants that if they elect a jury trial and lose, they can expect a much heftier sentence than if they agree to a plea bargain. This is done to try to dispose of cases through plea bargaining, out of fear of larger sentences, to alleviate as much of the case docket as possible—leaving fewer cases requiring a judge and jury for trial. Defense attorneys in Baltimore know that prosecutors are human; they can only try so many cases per day. A good defense attorney will spend significant time "educating" the prosecutor about the weaknesses in the case in the hopes of a favorable deal.

As a result, many cases, some involving serious charges like narcotics distribution, resolve with a guilty plea and a suspended jail sentence. Some sentences are even more lenient, such as a monetary fine.

Compare that with the docket for Kent County. There, prosecutors arrive for court confident there will be judges and jurors for every case to be tried. Consequently, they evaluate whether to try a case based on the likelihood of winning, the basis by which most lawyers determine whether to try cases or settle them. That same drug distribution defendant who took a plea with a suspended sentence in Baltimore City is looking at a two-year prison sentence in Kent County even with a plea. The playing fields are completely different. Therefore, the effect of the accused's constitutional rights on the efficacy of the judicial system differs from one jurisdiction to another. This result is ironic since the purpose of guarantees such as the right to counsel is to level the playing field, not to make some fields far more favorable to the defendant.

Ultimately, the punishment for a given offense is much less in larger populated, higher crime areas than in lesser populated, lower crime areas. The problems highlighted here for

Baltimore City are not unique to Baltimore. They are to be found in courthouses across the country in major cities. Similar situations can be found in Cook County, Illinois, where Chicago is the epicenter, and in Harris County, Texas, where Houston handles far more cases than the surrounding areas.

In cities like these, teams responsible for prosecuting crimes must identify cases that need special attention to ensure that they are properly prepared, tried, and supervised. Projects like Baltimore's "War Room" allow state and local agencies to work together to achieve this goal. But even this carefully coordinated approach can fail under the pressure of huge numbers of cases and limited administrative resources.

Take, for example, former Baltimore City Deputy State's Attorney Page Croyder's comments when the War Room was created:

> *"It's not as though I don't understand how we've gotten here: Volume is what's gotten us here. We devalue cases. What the system is saying is we aren't going to bother as long as you're not bad enough. For example, a police officer caught two men in the act of stomping a victim into unconsciousness. A district court judge 'inexplicably' dismissed the felony assault at the preliminary hearing, making the charges misdemeanor second-degree assaults,"* Croyder said. *"One of the two arrestees was 'backing up nine years'—that is, he had nine years of a suspended sentence yet to serve on an armed robbery conviction,"* she said. *"The felony Assistant State's Attorney handed the case off to an inexperienced misdemeanor Assistant State's Attorney who nolle prossed it (elected to no longer prosecute) when the victim failed to show, and both defendants walked,"* Croyder said. *"We kind of let the case fall apart after the judge dismissed the felony.*

The judge dismissed the felony, the victim didn't show up: I don't think those are acceptable excuses. We should have marshaled our resources to prevent that outcome."[95]

Exhibit 1: MARYLAND CRIMINAL SENTENCES ON AVERAGE			
Crime	Maximum Sentence	State of Maryland Average Sentence	Baltimore City Average Sentence
Drug Possession	4 years (Non-marijuana)	1.3 years	0.16 years
Rape/Sexual Assault	Life (1st degree); 20 years (2nd degree)	24.3 years	9.6 years
Burglary	20 years (1st degree); 15 years (2nd degree)	4.6 years	2.5 years
Shoplifting or Robbery	15 years	8.7 years	7.0 years

---

[95] "Baltimore's War Room: A Work In Progress," The *Daily Record* (May 28, 2004).

ERIC D. OBERER

CHAPTER TWELVE

Mounting a Defense

"A man has to live with himself, and he should see to it that he always has good company." [96]

WITHIN A CRIMINAL JUSTICE SYSTEM that produces widely varying results from county to county, jurisdiction to jurisdiction, there are the criminal defense attorneys. Public defenders practice exclusively in the county to which they are assigned. Even many lawyers in private practice focus on one or two counties, learning the lay of the land there and rarely venturing outside it. Public defenders, however, are generally buried beneath a crushing caseload. Defendants who can afford to pay for a lawyer in private practice could receive substantially more "justice" than those who exercise their right to appointed counsel at the state's expense.

A private lawyer might have one or two trials to handle in a day. A prosecutor might have fifteen or thirty. The same goes for a public defender, often tasked with representing most of the defendants on the docket. Guess which of these lawyers will have had the most time, focus, energy, and, often, budgeted

---

[96] Justice Charles Evan Hughes (1930–1941).

funds[97] to prepare a case?

Defense attorneys understand this landscape, and they exploit it as much as possible. If you want to see how the justice system really functions, get to court about thirty minutes early. The conversations that take place then, between the prosecutor and the defense lawyers before the judge even takes the bench, determine which cases will be tried, which will be postponed or moved to the stet docket, and which will be resolved by a plea. Defense lawyers jockey for position against one another, each hoping for a favorable deal based on the fact that other defendants might have to have their cases heard that day.

Another tactic involves requests for postponement in the hopes that the speedy trial deadline will resolve the case when it is not tried in time. When the final deadline looms, if the prosecutor has to choose between trying a less serious offense and a serious one, particularly if it's a "War Room" case, the prosecutor will choose the serious one—and that might mean the less serious case gets dismissed. Or it might mean a sweetheart deal involving probation or even a simple fine. Private lawyers are able to command exorbitant fees for knowing how to play this game.

But for the victims of the crimes that lead to these trials, it's no game. Many wind up feeling disgusted, dispirited, and angry. They came to court ready and willing to testify; they did what the state asked of them, and nothing seemed to come of it. Criminals return to the streets to offend again.

What makes an unjust system even more unjust? In the next section, the human element of our criminal justice system will be analyzed—the police, defense attorneys, prosecutors, and judges.

---

[97] Cases aren't always won by legal acumen alone. In some cases, the testimony of expert witnesses will determine guilt or innocence, sanity or insanity. Expert witnesses charge hundreds of dollars per hour for their time.

PART FOUR

BROKEN JUSTICE:
THE HUMAN ELEMENT

"Decency, security and liberty alike demand that government officials shall be subjected to the same rules of conduct that are commands to the citizen. In a government of laws, existence of the government will be imperiled if it fails to observe the law scrupulously."
—**Louis Brandeis**, Supreme Court Justice (1916-1939)
Olmstead v. United States, 277 U.S. 438, 485 (1928)

CHAPTER THIRTEEN

When Cops Go Bad

"The young man knows the rules,
but the old man knows the exceptions." [98]

THE GUN TRACE TASK FORCE: It was a good idea... until it wasn't.

Baltimore police are in a bind. While there is no excuse for turning to unethical and criminal activity, their pay is not commensurate with the level of risk they undertake and the sacrifices the job requires. Officers watch their arrests bargained away for peanuts in Baltimore's courthouses. There is an old saying among Baltimore cops: "I have the number for the State's Attorney's Office...just dial 443-set-them-free."

When the Baltimore City Police Department created the Gun Trace Task Force (the GTTF), it was intended to be an elite squad of highly trained officers tasked with seizing illegal guns. Instead, the officers went rogue and used their power to steal money, drugs, and guns, terrorizing people along the way. In some cases, they re-sold the drugs and guns they seized and therefore returned them to the streets they were supposedly cleaning up.

---

[98] Justice Oliver Wendell Holmes (1902–1932).

A lengthy investigation headed by the FBI determined that members of the GTTF committed robberies and extortion, and made false claims for overtime they hadn't worked.[99] Most of the officers eventually pled guilty to the charges that were filed against them. This included Sergeant Wayne Jenkins, a one-time rising star within the department who led the task force beginning in 2016. Two of the officers stood trial in proceedings that were humiliating for the department and for the City of Baltimore.

Jenkins's conduct was, to many, astonishing. It was not for nothing that Police Commissioner Kevin Clark remarked that the GTTF had operated like members of a 1930s-style gang. Jenkins stole drugs from the suspects the GTTF targeted, then fenced the drugs through a bail bondsman with whom he shared the profits. He and other members of the team pocketed cash seized during searches; if a suspect was arrested carrying $5,000 in cash on his person, officers might log $2,000 or $3,000 as evidence and then pocket the rest. What was the arrestee going to do? He couldn't prove how much cash he'd been carrying because drug dealers don't maintain business records.

In one case that was described at trial, Jenkins and his men broke open a safe owned by a suspect and found $200,000 and several kilos of cocaine inside. The men removed half of the money and some of the cocaine, then resealed the safe and faked a cellphone video as they reopened it to find the manipulated "contents" inside, which were dutifully logged. Another man went to prison because Jenkins planted drugs on him.

The GTTF was able to operate smoothly because it maintained relationships with criminals. One of its members, Detective Momodu Gondo, had grown up with a man who was a

---

[99] Jessica Lussenhop, "Who Were the Corrupt Baltimore Police Officers?" BBC News, Baltimore (Feb. 13, 2018), https://www.bbc.com/news/world-us-canada-43035628.

member of a heroin-dealing organization and the two of them shared information to each other's benefit. Gondo also used police tracking equipment to determine when a robbery target was not at home so that he could steal drugs, weapons, and other valuables. On another occasion, Gondo and another officer held a woman at gunpoint while they robbed her home. Another member of the task force, Sergeant Thomas Allers, stole money during a search of a suspect's home. The suspect was later murdered because the stolen money left the man unable to pay a drug-related debt. The men kept BB guns in their cruisers in case they needed to plant a weapon to justify having shot a suspect.

Tellingly, members of the GTTF told investigators that they frequently used "door pops" to generate arrests. In a "door pop," officers pull their car into a crowded area and then "pop" open the doors. As soon as anyone in the crowd tried to run away, officers would chase them down and arrest them. In this way, the Broken Windows policing theory became a conduit for corruption in the police force. The team was praised because it generated so many arrests and seizures, and the more praise came in, the bigger the officers' egos got. As the investigation was nearing its conclusion, some of the officers had even gotten wind of it, and yet they did not stop. There was a sense within the team that they were untouchable. That sentiment can almost certainly be traced, at least in part, to the power police departments accrued under years of Broken Windows-inspired policies.

The truth about the GTTF was finally revealed once the officers were arrested in a sting operation organized by the FBI, the DOJ, and state officials. On one level, the information had long been known by members of the communities patrolled by the BPD. Activists and others complained for years about discriminatory tactics employed in patrolling Black neighborhoods. They were vindicated once the news circulated.

These facts, however, have done nothing to improve the relationship between the City Police Department and the communities it serves. The population no longer seeks to cooperate with police, and jurors from those communities no longer trust the testimony of police officers at trial.

Finally, the collapse of the GTTF means that hundreds of convictions obtained based on the officers' testimony or evidence had to be re-examined. Convictions deemed tainted because the officers may have lied or planted evidence are being challenged now by defense attorneys, and many are being vacated. The passage of time never works in the state's favor. Witnesses die or move away, and physical evidence is lost or destroyed. It is possible that guilty people have already been or will be released from prison and returned to the community because of the GTTF. More than eighty convictions have been overturned due to GTTF misconduct, and over 800 more are being investigated.[100]

---

[100] Matthew Clarke, "The Role of Police Misconduct in Wrongful Convictions," Criminal Legal News (Aug. 19, 2019), https://www.criminallegal news.org/news/2019/aug/19/role-police-misconduct-wrongful-convictions/.

CHAPTER FOURTEEN

When Attorneys Go Bad

"[A]ny lawyer worth his salt will tell the suspect in no uncertain terms to make no statement to the police under any circumstances." [101]

IN BALTIMORE, THE TEMPTATION to cross the proverbial line always exists, as I am sure it does wherever there is illicit money to be made. One day, when I was a rookie prosecutor, I stepped out of the East Side District Courthouse and was approached by a man who suggested that he could send a lot of money my way. All he needed from me was my assurance that charges against him and his crew would never go anywhere. I ignored him and later reported the incident to a supervisor. Apparently, that sort of thing happens pretty often. My supervisor barely gave it any thought.

I had worked too hard and read too many cases in law school to sell out that easily. But I could also recognize how seductive the offer might be for someone demoralized or disillusioned by a failing system. If justice is never really on offer, why bother working long hours for relatively little money?

---

[101] Justice Robert H. Jackson, *Watts v. Indiana*, 228 U.S. 49 (1949) (concurring).

This is not to say that all defense attorneys are dishonest or unethical; far from it. Many take their obligations as officers of the court and as advocates very seriously. But there are certainly lucrative deals to be made, and I had the opportunity to work with some attorneys who made exceedingly poor decisions. Two of them were Stanley Needleman and Kenneth Ravenell.

The Stanley Needleman Case

Stanley Needleman had practiced law for forty years when he went to prison for tax evasion. The sixty-nine-year-old attorney was one of Baltimore's most prominent criminal defense attorneys at the time of his conviction for tax evasion in 2011. He got caught in one of the oldest traps in the Drug Enforcement Administration's arsenal: he under-reported his income on his tax returns.

This was no minor oversight on his part. Needleman omitted $1.5 million of income over five years. He was able to do that because he represented clients engaged in the narcotics trade, and his clients paid him in cash. Every day Needleman placed his clients' fee payments into an envelope and personally walked the money to a bank. Needleman's office staff were kept in the dark. He and only he handled the money. The next morning, he brought back the bank envelope, empty and ready to be refilled.

Agents associated with the DEA became suspicious. A source came forward in 2007 with information about the attorney's cash, and there were rumors that Needleman was pocketing a lot of it. Federal agents were able to review Needleman's tax returns for the five-year period. They compared the sums the lawyer reported as income on his returns with the fees they estimated he earned in court cases, knowing the going rate for a lawyer of Needleman's experience and reputation. They were also able to speak with some of Needleman's former clients. The clients told the agents what they paid the lawyer, and once the agents had that information, they concluded that he wasn't being honest with the IRS about his earnings.

The DEA was issued search warrants for Needleman's home and office. They recovered two safes containing around $1.5 million in cash as well as handwritten ledgers accounting for fees received from clients. It also became clear that Needleman had been depositing his money in sums small enough not to trigger government attention. With that evidence in hand, it was fairly straightforward to charge him with several counts of tax fraud. Additionally, Needleman was disbarred, meaning he would no longer be able to practice law, and he was sentenced to a year in prison. He appeared for sentencing before a federal judge he had known professionally for many years, except that Needleman was usually seated at the table reserved for attorneys, and on this occasion, he was instead the accused.

Highly respected lawyers and judges vouched for his character in a bid to win him a reduced sentence. One was retired Baltimore County Circuit Court Judge Dana Levitz. "I always found him completely honest," he said in a hearing before Judge Roger W. Titus of the federal court. "I remember thinking how difficult it must be for him to be so zealous an advocate for such difficult clients. His total commitment, his total involvement—the practice of law was, for him, his sole focus."[102] Other character witnesses included Andrew Jay Graham, William Purpura, former Police Commissioner Ed Norris, and Judge Joseph F. Murphy, who had been chief judge of

---

[102] Edward Ericson, Jr., "Attorney Stanley Needleman Sentenced to a Year in Prison," The *Baltimore Sun* (June 4, 2014), https://www.baltimore sun.com/citypaper/bcp-blog-11584-20111215-story.html.

the Maryland Court of Appeals for many years.

Judge Titus refused the federal prosecutor's request to enhance Needleman's sentence beyond the statutory minimum. But his attorneys had asked the court to order probation only, so the court's inclusion of jail time represented a compromise. Many were surprised that he was required to serve time at all. Former City Circuit Court judge and respected attorney William H. "Billy" Murphy told reporters that he thought Needleman would win the day.[103] Many believe that Judge Titus relied on information that was not made public in sentencing Needleman.

The charges that brought down this once prominent member of the Maryland bar concerned taxes, but there was speculation at the time that Needleman was involved in far more serious offenses. For example, in 2007, he provided $30,000 to bail out one of his clients, Jose Morales. Once released, Morales attempted to charter a flight from Texas back to Baltimore to transport six kilos of cocaine. That much cocaine has a street value of around $180,000. Morales told police he had to sell the cocaine in order to pay back a bail bond. He also told them his attorney was involved in criminal activities.

Although Morales was sentenced in Texas, federal prosecutors brought him to Maryland to face additional conspiracy charges. The nature of the charges against him was vague. The judge who heard the case was Judge Titus. We now know that Morales was facing a number of charges around Maryland in 2008 and was being represented by Needleman when a long-time associate of Morales, Robert Long, agreed to turn state's evidence—meaning he would testify against Morales. Long was murdered two weeks later. Another man was convicted of the slaying, but Needleman, who did not represent any of the parties involved, visited court that day to hear the guilty

---

[103] *Id.*

verdict. It was strange that a man who could charge hundreds of dollars an hour, who would have had a great deal of work to be done, would take the time to attend a proceeding for which he could expect to earn no fee. Nevertheless, he was never charged with any crime related to the death of Long.

The Kenneth Ravenell Case

Stanley Needleman was represented by another well-respected, highly experienced Baltimore criminal defense lawyer: Kenneth Ravenell. Ten years later, Ravenell was himself indicted by the federal government for crimes committed in the course of his professional duties.[104] The charges against Ravenell alleged far more involvement in narcotics activity. According to the government, he actively laundered money and obstructed justice for the clients he represented.

For example, according to the attorneys representing the United States, Ravenell personally visited a restaurant parking lot to make a handoff of cash. He also traveled to a Four Seasons hotel in Atlanta for a meeting to discuss drug money. On another occasion, Ravenell claimed to represent a man who was being held in jail. Based on that representation, he was permitted to meet with the man. However, during the meeting, the two did not discuss legal issues; instead, Ravenell sought information about money owed to Ravenell's client, a drug kingpin named Richard Byrd.

As in the Needleman investigation, federal agents obtained sealed warrants for accounting records maintained by Ravenell's law firm. Nearly $2 million made its way through the firm,

---

[104] "Federal indictment offers new details of Baltimore attorney Ravenell's alleged scheme to help drug kingpin," The *Baltimore Sun* (Jan. 9, 2021), https://baltimoresun.newspapers.com/image/708483412/?terms=ravenell &match=1/.

with about $630,000 of it retained as legal fees. Some of the money made its way to a Florida property development company that was managed by a Baltimore man and a Texas lawyer who also eventually pled guilty to laundering money for Byrd.

The indictment against Ravenell suggests that his involvement was not confined to Maryland. In 2013, according to the government, Ravenell sent a private investigator to meet with the owner of a shipping company. The investigator, who posed as a law enforcement officer in order to gain access to the witness, was instructed to find out what the witness could tell investigators about Byrd. Ravenell sent another investigator to meet with a man in Texas in the hopes that the man would provide a statement refuting any involvement with Byrd. The man refused to do so. And in July 2014, Ravenell went to Atlanta on a mission for Byrd, who by then was under indictment.

Other lawyers associated with Ravenell's law firm denied any involvement. According to a report in the *Baltimore Sun,* those lawyers stated that they had not made investments with Byrd's money. "My father and I have always acted legally and ethically in all of our dealings," a representative of the firm said. "We have not been charged with any crime, and it would be inappropriate for us to further comment about pending litigation in which we are not a party."[105] Ravenell left that law firm in 2014 after it was raided by the DEA and the IRS.

Ravenell was convicted in December 2021 of conspiracy to commit money laundering. But the jury acquitted him of racketeering conspiracy and narcotics conspiracy charges. [106]

---

[105] *Id.*

[106] "Federal Jury Convicts Baltimore Defense Attorney for Money Laundering Conspiracy" (Dec. 28, 2021), https://www.justice.gov/usao-md/pr/federal-jury-convicts-baltimore-defense-attorney-money-laundering-conspiracy.

CHAPTER FIFTEEN

The Jury and Bias

*"Justice? You get justice in the next world.
In this world you have the law."* [107]

THE GUN TRACE TASK FORCE case is not the only example of police corruption, and it will not likely be the last. Further, the public's distrust of even honest police officers has been fed by years of Broken Windows-style policing efforts. When citizens report for jury duty, they bring this distrust with them.

Hindsight Is 20/20

When I was in my first year as a prosecutor, I was assigned to the Baltimore City District Court. The district court handles mostly misdemeanors, felony screenings or preliminary hearings, and small civil claims. Once a defendant demands a jury trial, his or her case is transferred to the circuit court. I was assigned to handle the misdemeanor docket during the O'Malley era of zero-tolerance policing. There, I saw firsthand the effects of that policy, and I learned how devastating the effects were for the courts.

---

[107] William Gaddis. *A Frolic of His Own.* Scribner (1994).

A Juror Predisposed

I later arrived at the Circuit Court to try cases before juries. Now I was reaping what had been sown, trying to select jurors who would be willing to trust police officers. I remember one case in particular in which the victim had been robbed of a great deal of money. The case had been scheduled *four separate times* for trial, and the defendant's attorney obtained a postponement each time.

Finally, the case was set for trial. By the time the judge called for jurors, only twenty potential jurors were still available to serve. The rest had been selected for other trials. During *voir dire*, eight of the potential jurors were disqualified or stricken for various reasons. We were then left with twelve potential jurors. One of them announced that he would never find in favor of the State because he "hated the police" and "would never believe anything they said." The victim in the case told me that if the case was postponed a fifth time, she would not show up and that she was fed up with the process.

My options were to dismiss the case or try it with a jury that included a man who would outright refuse to convict. I decided to try it. What did I have to lose? If the case was dismissed, the State and the victim would certainly receive no recourse. If I tried it, there was at least a chance I could change the man's mind.

I did my best. Not only did he hold out, but he also convinced everybody else on the jury to vote with him to acquit.

The CSI Effect

In our legal system, to convict a person of a crime, the state must prove the person's guilt beyond a reasonable doubt. For centuries, that has been the standard of proof. Within the last fifty years or so, science and technology have made huge leaps forward. On the one hand, that is an incredibly positive development for criminal justice. Crimes have been solved, sometimes many years later, because evidence collected at the scene yielded a DNA match. On the other hand, there is a downside.

Jurors arrive for trial with preconceived ideas and opinions, and recently, those preconceived ideas often concern scientific evidence. The public has heard a lot about it. They watch crime and courtroom procedurals on television. They listen to true crime podcasts. The extremely popular NPR podcast, *Serial,* actually focused on a crime in Baltimore. Another popular television show, *CSI: Crime Scene Investigation*, made celebrities out of crime scene techs. Every week, viewers could tune in to watch a group of good-looking people work in an aesthetically designed laboratory surrounded by a lot of expensive-looking equipment. I probably don't have to tell you, although maybe I do, that real crime labs don't look like that.

A lot of people are watching these shows. In 2006, for example, an average of forty million people tuned in to watch *CSI: Crime Scene Investigation*. And that number doesn't even account for viewers of the many other similarly themed shows like *Cold Case, Numb3rs*, and *NCIS*.[108]

Now seems like a good time to remind you that prosecutors won cases for several hundred years before DNA was even discovered. How did they do that? They relied on other kinds of evidence, like witness testimony, which is an example of what lawyers call direct evidence. They also relied on indirect or circumstantial evidence. Defense lawyers sometimes suggest that circumstantial evidence is bad or unreliable. In some cases, it can be. But it isn't always, and if there's enough of it, it's perfectly appropriate for a jury to convict a defendant

---

[108] Honorable Donald E. Shelton, "The 'CSI Effect,' Does It Really Exist?" *The National Institute of Justice Journal* (March 16, 2008), https://nij.ojp .gov/topics/articles/csi-effect-does-it-really-exist.

based on circumstantial evidence alone, no matter what a defense lawyer says in the closing argument on *Law & Order*.

Many potential jurors are, at this point, so saturated with crime fiction that they forget crime facts. They wait for the prosecutor to produce the DNA evidence, the fiber evidence, the fingerprints, and the shoe prints. They expect the prosecutor to do that because prosecutors on television are always doing it. In reality, that kind of evidence isn't always available or can't always be tested reliably. It's possible and even likely, though, that juries are acquitting guilty people because they think prosecutors haven't proven their cases, and they think the cases weren't proven because they didn't see any DNA evidence. Commenters have called this the *"CSI Effect."*

In 2006, two criminology professors surveyed 1,000 prospective jurors about their evidentiary expectations. The idea was to see if the CSI Effect is real and, if so, how it was shaping these jurors' assumptions about evidence and trials. Surveyors inquired about different kinds of cases (murder, rape, burglary, weapons crimes, and so on) and what kind of evidence jurors expected to be shown (eyewitness testimony, DNA evidence, fingerprint evidence, ballistics, and so on). Then the jurors were asked how likely it was that they would find a defendant guilty, given the kinds of evidence presented. The results were startling.

Forty-six percent of participants said they expected to be shown some kind of scientific evidence in every criminal case. Twenty-two percent expected that prosecutors would offer DNA evidence in every criminal case. Thirty-six percent expected fingerprint evidence in every criminal case, and thirty-two percent believed that ballistics or other firearms-type evidence would be offered in every criminal case. Every. Single. Case.

But that's not all. The criminologists also discovered that the jurors' expectations were different depending on the kind of case. More people thought that DNA evidence was essential in serious violent crimes like murder or rape. (This makes some sense; those are the kinds of crimes in which the offenders are more likely to leave bodily fluids behind.) They expected that fingerprint evidence would be offered in breaking and entering cases, theft cases, and weapons crimes.[109]

Surveyors also asked respondents about the specific shows they watched and how realistic they believed those shows to be. The results suggest the jurors are watching shows like *CSI: Crime Scene Investigation* a lot, and they expect the evidence offered in the trials they attend to look like what they've seen on television. If it doesn't, the state risks a loss.

A Case of Jury Bias?

I experienced the "*CSI Effect*" personally. I was trying a "War Room" offender who refused a plea. He was charged with conspiracy to distribute narcotics and possession. I had no choice but to try it and hope for a conviction and maximum sentence.

Three detectives told the jury that they had watched the defendant lift up a can in an alley, take out small bags of heroin, and then bring those bags to purchasers. After several of these transactions, one of the detectives arrested a purchaser and took possession of the heroin. Another detective arrested the defendant, and the third seized the stash of heroin in the alley. The detective who arrested the dealer also found a small baggie of another narcotic in the defendant's coat, probably for his personal use.

At trial, I entered all of the narcotics into evidence. I called the detectives as eyewitnesses, I called technicians to establish that the substances hadn't been changed from the time they

---

[109] *Id.*

were seized until the time they were tested, and I called the chemist who tested them and determined that they were illegal narcotics. The defense attorney began his cross-examination. He had a copy of a 300-page manual of procedures for the City Police Department. He had found, buried inside, a single, tiny paragraph that suggested that drugs be fingerprinted. This was not a requirement. It was a "best practices" suggestion.

Mind you, I had been to the Crime Lab's fingerprint analysis room many times before this trial. I observed how fingerprinting was done. To my astonishment, it was done manually. The technician visually compared the defendant's fingerprints with fingerprints found on a piece of evidence. There were no enormous neon-lit LCD screens, no holograms. The procedure looked nothing like what you'd expect if you watched a lot of crime shows. In any event, considering the number of drug seizures occurring in Baltimore every day, there was and still is no way to fingerprint all of them. There aren't enough employees or enough hours in the day.

Was that omission enough to create reasonable doubt? After all, we had three credible detectives testify about what they saw. That should have been plenty. But we also had a jury that expected forensic evidence. Individual jurors could also very well have had negative experiences with the police. One reason jurors might demand forensic evidence, in fact, might be their distrust of police officers.

The jury returned a compromise verdict. It found the defendant guilty of possession of the narcotic found in his coat pocket but not guilty of conspiracy to distribute the heroin, which was the much more serious charge. After the trial, I found myself in the elevator with one of the jurors. She wanted to discuss the case with me, and she told me that she felt the state should have given the jury more evidence. I don't know what else we could have given them, but prosecutors everywhere are dealing with similar issues.

CHAPTER SIXTEEN

Our Misperceptions

*"At his best, man is the noblest of all animals;
separated from law and justice, he is the worst."* [110]

THE CONSTITUTION IS DESIGNED to preserve and safe-guard individual liberties and rights. The Founding Fathers wanted these protections in place to avert any potential crises similar to what the New World had experienced with the British government by way of King George's empire. They spelled out individual rights as they pertain to criminal procedure in the Bill of Rights, as we have discussed:

- *Fourth Amendment*: The right to be protected from unreasonable searches and seizures.
- *Fifth Amendment*: The right to a grand jury, freedom against double jeopardy, and freedom from self-incrimination.
- *Sixth Amendment*: The right to assistance of counsel; the right to a trial by an impartial jury; the right to confront witnesses; and the right to a speedy and public trial.

---

[110] Aristotle. *The Philosophy of Aristotle*. Mass Market Paperback (2011).

- *Eighth Amendment*: Freedom from excessive bail and cruel and unusual punishment.
- *Fourteenth Amendment*: Freedom from deprivation of life, liberty, and property without due process of law or equal protection under the law; application of the foregoing rights to the states.

These fundamental rights directly impact the ability of the criminal justice system to mete out justice as that word is generally understood by American citizens. The many disparities resulting from the preservation of these rights to the exclusion of other concerns mean that the system rarely achieves equal justice under the law.

Administrating a system that protects all the rights afforded under the Constitution is not only impractical but also impossible when jurisdictions have vastly different crime rates, types of crime, and resources available to fight them. Those fundamental rights directly impact the ability of the criminal justice system to mete out justice as that word is generally understood by America's citizens. "*Equal* Justice Under Law" is often frustrated by the administration of the justice system in the local counties of each respective state of this country...because it is inherently *unequal*. The same fundamental rights apply in rural and lower crime areas as they do in urban and higher crime areas. As a consequence, urban areas see a lower rate of convictions and shorter sentences for the same crimes occurring therein than their rural counterparts due to their inability to have enough judges and jurors to provide each individual accused of a crime with their fundamental rights to a speedy trial by jury.

Baltimore City could arguably move many more cases through the system if it hired more judges and court employees and built a new courthouse. But can you really bring thousands of citizens in each day for jury duty? The existing Circuit

Court courthouses are, frankly, decrepit. The walls and ceilings are crumbling in places. There is lead in the paint and asbestos in the drywall. The design of the buildings themselves leaves much to be desired; each of the courthouses is a remnant of a different time when sculpted plaster on the ceilings mattered, and court files were handwritten by clerks. Trying a case now, with lawyers' laptops, the courtroom clerk's recording equipment, and audio-visual equipment, is a nightmare of tangled electrical cords and spotty WiFi access. All of these problems, in combination with the ones we have already discussed, render the system currently unworkable.

Addressing these issues is complicated. In Baltimore, Mayor O'Malley's Broken Windows policy in the early 2000s seemed effective at first but came at a significant cost. Fast forward twenty years and the most recent Baltimore City State's Attorney, Marilyn Mosby, elected not to prosecute certain misdemeanor crimes like simple drug possession, prostitution, and minor traffic offenses.[111] Mosby justifies this policy by claiming that it decreases the number of negative interactions between police officers and citizens. The newly elected Baltimore City State's Attorney—Ivan Bates—promises to strike a balance between the policies of the aforementioned prior administrations.

Will this contribute to a less cynical jury pool in the future? Mosby's policy does free up courtrooms and jurors, making resources available for serious crimes. But it means that petty crimes will go unpunished. If you get to work or school by bicycle and you have to keep replacing your stolen bikes, you might not be happy to know that no one cares. The Mosby

---

[111] Ted Prudente, "Mosby Policies Explained," The *Baltimore Sun* (Apr. 26, 2021), https://www.baltimoresun.com/news/crime/bs-pr-md-ci-cr-mosby-policies-explained-20210426-wgpds7ccbjgitlj3bibpkhxrpi-sto-y.html#:~:text=What%20else%20won%27t%20be,urinating%20and%20defecating%20in%20public.

approach may send that signal, unfortunately: that non-violent crimes don't matter. Its efficacy as a crime-fighting and resource-distribution tool will be determined over the next few years. It seems a well-intentioned effort to repair the community-law enforcement relationship.

When the words "Equal *Justice* Under Law" are inscribed prominently above the entrance to the highest court in the land, the expectation is for the type of *justice* the word connotes—that which is merited or deserved. Yet that type of justice competes directly with a higher institutional principle—to protect the innocent from being wrongly convicted of crimes. The two concepts cannot co-exist without some level of conflict. The protection of the individual's rights in a given case can produce results that are not what the public understands as "just," as we have seen in many famous cases and as we see every day in courtrooms throughout this great land. Those results, while difficult to understand on a case-by-case basis, are critical to ensuring that *everyone's* fundamental rights are not infringed upon.

Without a complete understanding of the American version of justice, but rather the expectation of *Merriam-Webster's* definition of justice, Americans are often frustrated. That frustration often has grave consequences. That misunderstanding and frustration therewith have existed for decades, if not longer. Civil unrest and rioting have been commonplace in this country since long before the 1960s through the present time that is chronicled in this book.

The United States is a country that holds itself out as—and even explicitly states that it is—a country of "Equal Justice Under Law." But the protection of individual liberties and rights puts that ideal in the backseat. The problem is not so much with the system of criminal justice that the Founding Fathers set up for the United States, but rather with the understanding—or shall we say, misunderstanding—of large numbers of its citizens.

Following the Rule of Law

The United States ranks twenty-first on a list of 128 countries based on adherence to the rule of law.[112] The World Justice Project (WJP) Rule of Law Index defines the rule of law as a durable system of laws, institutions, norms, and community commitment that upholds four universal principles:

1) **Accountability:** The government as well as private actors are accountable under the law.
2) **Just Laws:** The laws are clear, publicized, and stable, are applied evenly, and protect fundamental rights, including the security of persons and contract, property, and human rights.
3) **Open Government:** The processes by which the laws are enacted, administered, and enforced are accessible, fair, and efficient.
4) **Accessible and Impartial Dispute Resolution:** Justice is delivered timely by competent, ethical, and independent representatives and neutrals who are accessible, have adequate resources, and reflect the makeup of the communities they serve.[113]

---

[112] World Justice Project Rule of Law Index 2020, worldjusticeproject.org, https://worldjusticeproject.org/our-work/research-and-data/wjp-rule-law-index-2020. The twenty countries with greater adherence are Denmark, Norway, Finland, Sweden, the Netherlands, Germany, New Zealand, Austria, Canada, Estonia, Australia, Singapore, the United Kingdom, Belgium, Japan, Hong Kong, South Korea, the Czech Republic, Spain, and France (in that order). *See also* https://www.abajournal.com/news/article/us-falls-out-of-top-20-in-rule-of-law-index-while-overall-declines-continue.

[113] "WJP Insights 2020," worldjusticeproject.org, https://worldjusticeproject.org/sites/default/files/documents/WJP%20Insights%202020%20-%20Online%20.pdf.

In 2020, the WJP examined 128 countries using the following categories: constraints on government power, absence of corruption, open government, fundamental rights, order and security, regulatory enforcement, civil justice, and criminal justice. According to the study, these factors basically determine the effectiveness of a nation's justice system.[114] Points are assigned for each category, with higher scores indicating more adherence to the law. A score of 0 or 1 demonstrates a strong adherence to the rule of law. The United States scored 0.72, falling from its previous spot at No. 20 to No. 21, just below France and Spain. The United States was ranked No. 22 for criminal justice,[115] No. 28 for order and security,[116] and No. 19 for the absence of corruption.[117] However, a strong rule of law

---

[114] "World Justice Project Rule of Law Index 2020," worldjusticeproject.org, https://worldjusticeproject.org/sites/default/files/documents/WJP-ROLI-2020-Online_0.pdf.

[115] Criminal Justice (Factor 8) "evaluates a country's criminal justice system. An effective criminal justice system is a key aspect of the rule of law, as it constitutes the conventional mechanism to redress grievances and bring action against individuals for offenses against society. An assessment of the delivery of criminal justice should take into consideration the entire system, including the police, lawyers, prosecutors, judges, and prison officers." World Justice Project Rule of Law Index 2020, *supra*.

[116] Order and Security (Factor 5) "measures how well a society ensures the security of persons and property. Security is one of the defining aspects of any rule of law society and is a fundamental function of the state. It is also a precondition for the realization of the rights and freedoms that the rule of law seeks to advance." World Justice Project Rule of Law Index 2020, *supra*.

[117] Corruption (Factor 2) "measures the absence of corruption in government. The factor considers three forms of corruption: bribery, improper influence by public or private interests, and misappropriation of public funds or other resources. These three forms of corruption are examined with respect to government officers in the executive branch, the judiciary, the military, police, and the legislature." World Justice Project Rule of Law Index 2020, *supra*.

does not mean ensuring a state of justice. The rule of law in the United States requires compliance with the Fifth Amendment, for example. Did Lizzie Borden get away with murder? Might the result have been different if she had been confronted at trial with statements she made while she was in custody? Would O.J. Simpson have been convicted if he had not been represented by a "dream team" of lawyers? I guess we'll never really know. Maybe we will never be able to agree on what "proof beyond a reasonable doubt" requires. Very few cases can be proven with exactitude. The families of Ronald Goldman and Caylee Anthony will probably never receive the justice they deserve.

Can the Misperception Be Rectified?

As we have seen in the cases summarized in this book, and as we see every day in courtrooms throughout the country, these so-called "unjust" results—while difficult to understand on a case-by-case basis—are critical to ensuring that *everyone's* fundamental rights are preserved.

Without a complete understanding of the American version of justice, relying exclusively on *Merriam-Webster's* definition of justice, Americans are often left frustrated, dismayed, and angry. Those feelings can lead to grave consequences. The inability to reconcile what we believe to be the meaning of "justice" with what we eventually receive from our justice system has led to violence, bloodshed, and extraordinary damage to businesses and property.

There are real and significant reasons for the American public's dissatisfaction with the criminal justice system. Many people are clamoring for change. They believe that there must be a better way of reconciling individual rights with what is good for society as a whole.

We must continue striving to inform and educate our citizens about why the system works the way it does. Even if it is flawed—and it surely is—it is still one of the best systems in the world.

We have long reassured ourselves that American justice is the best form of justice available. That conviction is called into question, at the very least, by the results of the WJP's rule of law index. Perhaps we have things to learn from other democratic nations. Is that preferable to re-aligning the expectations of the American public as a way to lower frustration?

Can you imagine if everyone in the United States grew up understanding the limitations of our justice system yet understood what we are striving for as a society—that is, protections from the governmental tyranny that led to the violent overthrowing of the prior government during the American Revolutionary War? Imagine a complete paradigm shift in understanding and thinking about our justice system. Imagine if all Americans fully understood that, sometimes, justice means applying the law through "courts of law" that safeguard everyone in society against the potential for governmental tyranny, even if those results are not fully just in individual cases. Imagine if the demand for the perfect application of the law through "courts of justice" were replaced with an understanding that while not always "just" in individual results in a given case, such results are necessary to holistically protect *all* Americans from the very dangers the U.S. Constitution was set up to protect against. If there truly were this widespread paradigm shift in the understating of the masses, I believe there would be more satisfaction in our justice system and less dissent—even less civil unrest.

But is educating the public enough? Questions remain. Was our system established for a smaller population but is now overwhelmed? Was it designed for a time when there was less crime per capita than there is today? Is there a better system elsewhere that we could model?

Would there be less retaliation crime in the United States if assailants were convicted at higher rates? Police and prosecutors often compete with those that had a relationship with a murdered decedent in trying to provide justice. Many times, before the police and prosecutors can even locate or let alone bring an assailant before a jury, the assailant known in the community has been the victim of a retribution murder. Frequently, that is how justice is dispensed outside of courtrooms in the United States. Many citizens take the law into their own hands because they know that proof of guilt beyond a reasonable doubt in a courtroom is often hard to obtain.

There are significant historical underpinnings of American dissatisfaction and frustration with what appears to be a widely held perception of unfairness and inefficiency in the American criminal justice system. Many in the United States are clamoring for change—even going as far as advocating for the complete defunding of the police. Is throwing the baby out with the bathwater the solution? That remains to be seen. But it does go to the heart of the problem: large numbers of Americans are frustrated with this country's justice system and have been for decades. The concept of justice that they understand—that is, merited or deserved results—often runs in direct opposition to the goal of protecting the plethora of fundamental rights of the accused. Something's got to give. Maybe it has been giving for decades—through widespread civil unrest and otherwise. Perhaps we should look to the other justice systems around the world that are rated higher in the rule of law. Or perhaps shifting the paradigm of the American public to understand the differences between their perceptions of the American justice system and the realities of the American justice system will be enough. Only time will tell.

A Tale of Two Johnnies

"As you discover what strength you can draw from your community in this world from which it stands apart, look outward as well as inward. Build bridges instead of walls." [118]

AS A CHILD, I became interested in how people treated each other and how our government treated its citizens. Growing up in one of the poorest, most crime-ridden counties in southwest Ohio, I was fortunate to have caring, forward-looking parents. Occasionally they considered moving, but it never really was an option. My parents told me, "Look, if you are going to grow up here, you are going to see how everyone lives." They were deeply empathetic people, and they encouraged me to follow in their footsteps. I learned from my parents that empathy is a muscle. If you work it regularly, it will grow strong. If you ignore it, it will atrophy.

I attended school for about half of my childhood in a very rural area. I spent the other half in a decaying industrial city affectionately referred to by locals as "Little Detroit"—Springfield, Ohio. At the time, it seemed crazy. But I grew to respect

---

[118] Justice Sonia Sotomayor. *My Beloved World*. Vintage (2014).

my parents' decision, for it forged in me a desire to think outside the box. I learned to see beyond my own little world and surroundings. I met a lot of great people, I met some people who were down on their luck, and I met some people who were downright lousy. Some of my classmates came from farming families, some lived in trailer parks, and others lived in the inner city.

I was told that not too many people from Springfield went to law school. I am grateful that I got to be one of the lucky few who did.

What I have learned is that good people come from all walks of life. Most of us want what is best for our children, sometimes make big mistakes, and want to be successful. Those dreams are achievable for some, but not all, of us. Setting expectations can lead to boom or bust stories like the tale of two Johnnies.

I had some *interesting* schoolmates in Clark County. John Stephens sat on my left in one class. He was very smart, into civics, and a good singer. Jon Carson sat on my right in a different classroom. The year I graduated from high school, Jon Carson was named a first-team All-Ohio basketball player. Scouts from all over the country were keeping an eye on him. He was thought by some to be one of the best guards in the country.

That year, I spent most of my afternoons volunteering at local city commissioners' meetings, tutoring kids at the Urban League, or working with John Stephens and others, helping the Springfield Area Youth Council form the city's first youth center. I played some basketball with Jon Carson at the YMCA, but more often, I watched him tear it up on his way to basketball stardom.

The lives of these two uber-talented classmates of mine took very divergent paths. You may have heard of John Stephens by now. He is a Grammy Award-winning singer and television personality who goes by the name of John Legend. You may not have heard of Jon Carson. He was shot and killed while committing a violent home invasion and burglary after dropping out of college on his basketball scholarship and returning to Springfield. Sadly, his younger brother, Olajuwon, was also killed by a Molotov cocktail.[119] These two polar-opposite paths unfolded before me. And both stories shake me to this very day—in ways both good and bad.

This story about the two Johnnies that were classmates of mine partially inspired me to write this book. People make choices in life. Jon Carson made his, and John Stephens—now known as John Legend—made his. Both were undeniably uber-talented. Frankly, it was pretty cool to be classmates with both of them. Yet their stories turned out drastically different. While there are many reasons for this, I do believe that what was taught and ingrained in them about our society was very different.

I really believe that good people come from all walks of life and want the best chances they can have in the country—one they are told is the best country in the world. Yet, that is not always what they get. Setting expectations that deviate from that can lead to boom or bust stories like this. What we are taught about our society, the opportunities it has, and how to make the most of those opportunities are essential to our outcomes as productive citizens. What we are taught about the wrongs against us and how they are righted is also critical. Expectations for fairness and justice that are not aligned with reality can cause great disappointment, discouragement, and even despair.

One of the biggest reasons for the success and high status in the world for the United States is the stability of laws that creates worldwide investment in this county. But if our

---

[119] *State v. Knight*, 2008 Ohio 4926, 2008 Ohio App. LEXIS 4132 (2008).

citizens do not know how our laws work on a basic level, how those laws affect their daily lives and even opportunities, and create a false expectation for fairness and justice, we will see more and more boom or bust stories like these. It can be devastating to the psyche and one's outlook on life to feel that one is being treated unfairly—particularly by our society's justice system. Certainly, having the highest court in the land etched with the words "Equal Justice Under Law" can be misleading, create false expectations, and downright disappointment and worse if not fully understood.

While Jon Carson and John Legend went in two different directions for a myriad of reasons, it was ultimately their mindset and approach to life in our society that led them down the paths they did with what was, inarguably, amazing talent. I miss Jon and wish he were still with us. I am proud of John and what he has accomplished.

APPENDIX

Honoring the Symbols of Justice

"The President and the Congress are all very well in their way. They can say what they think they think, but it rests with the Supreme Court to decide what they have really thought." [120]

LADY JUSTICE IS A blindfolded woman carrying a sword and a set of scales. Her statue can be found in courthouses across the United States. She is meant to symbolize fair and equal administration of the law without corruption, favor, greed, or prejudices. The blindfold represents objectivity and impartiality. Justice should be meted out without fear or favor, regardless of money, wealth, or power. The scales represent the weighing of evidence. The scales must tilt dramatically in favor of guilt before a person can be convicted of a crime. The sword represents punishment, signifying that justice can be swift and final. She holds the sword below the scales because evidence is required before punishment. The snake beneath

---

[120] Theodore Roosevelt. *In the Words of Theodore Roosevelt: Quotations from the Man in the Arena.* Cornell University (2012).

her foot represents evil and lies. The book is the law, the constitution from which all justice is administered.

A statue called THE SPIRIT OF JUSTICE stands on display along with its male counterpart, MAJESTY OF JUSTICE, in the Great Hall of the Robert F. Kennedy Department of Justice Building in Washington, D.C. She has an identical twin at Congress' Rayburn House Office Building.

CONTEMPLATION OF JUSTICE is situated to the left of the steps leading to the main entrance of the Supreme Court. A seated female figure reflects on a small figure of justice that she holds in her right hand. The figure of justice is blindfolded and cradles a set of scales in her arms.

Another depiction of justice is on the base of the lampposts located at the front of the Supreme Court Plaza facing First Street. She, like her counterparts, holds a sword and scales of justice.

JUSTICE WITHOUT A BLINDFOLD appears in one of the Supreme Court courtroom displays. Here, a robed Justice is the focus of the allegorical story of the battle of good versus evil. She looks determinedly in the direction of the forces of evil. Her posture is defiant, as if ready to do battle to protect the forces of good with her great sword. The sword remains sheathed, but her hand rests atop the hilt.

THE BOOK OF JUDGMENT appears in the East Pediment of the Supreme Court Building, representing learning, written knowledge, and judgment. In a few instances, the Latin word *lex*, law, is carved into the book. Such books are held by several lawgivers, including Confucius.

In the West Pediment, RESEARCH PAST studies a book. CONTEMPLATION OF JUSTICE has a book under her arm, and a small open book is at the center point of the doorframe above the main entrance. In the courtroom display, Muhammad, Hugo Grotius, and John Marshall are depicted holding books.

In the east panel, MAJESTY OF LAW rests his arm on a book, as does the figure of a judge. One of the reliefs on the bronze elevator doorframes incorporates an open book inscribed with "LEX."

Throughout the history of Western art, tablets have signified the law. This tradition is closely associated with Moses, who, according to the Book of Exodus, descended from Mount Sinai with two stone tablets inscribed with the Ten Commandments. Over time, the use of two tablets has become a symbol for the commandments and, more generally, ancient laws.

Moses appears with two tablets in three places at the Supreme Court building: in the south panel of the courtroom display, in the East Pediment, and in one of the Great Hall metopes.[121] Two tablets with the Roman numerals I–X appear on the support frame of the courtroom's bronze gates, on the lower interior panels of the courtroom doors, and in the hands of the figure representing "Law" carved in the Library woodwork.

A single tablet inscribed "LEX" is held by AUTHORITY OF LAW, located to the right of the front steps. A single block with the Roman numerals I–X is centrally located in the east panel of the courtroom display between MAJESTY OF LAW and POWER OF GOVERNMENT. The surrounding iconography includes a blazing sun and a bald eagle with spreading wings—a symbol of America.

Another symbol that recalls the ancient nature of written law is SCROLL OF LAW. Several figures are depicted in the building's architecture with scrolls in hand. In the East Pediment, SOLON holds a scroll, and in the West Pediment, RESEARCH PAST reads an open scroll alongside an urn filled with more scrolls.

In the panel of the Bronze Doors titled THE WESTMINSTER

---

[121] *Merriam-Webster Dictionary* defines metope as the space between two triglyphs of a Doric frieze often adorned with carved work.

STATUTE, one of the figures reads from a scroll. One of the metopes in the Great Hall depicts an owl, a symbol of wisdom, in front of an open scroll. In the courtroom display, scrolls are depicted with the figures of Lycurgus, King John, and Justinian.

Scrolls date back to ancient times. In ancient Egypt, scrolls were made from papyrus and were the first form of records. The scroll is closely associated with law and justice, signifying knowledge, learning, the extent of a life, and the passing of time. It also represents continued learning and education as a responsibility of society and everyone in it.

In the great gateway city of New York, symbols of justice greet all who visit. THE STATUE OF LIBERTY was a gift from France to the United States. It is meant to symbolize liberty and freedom. Implicit in the symbol of liberty is the promise of justice. Liberty and freedom cannot co-exist without justice for all members of society.

Depictions of blind justice or battles against good and evil would lead us to believe that the American justice system will deliver on this promise eventually, as if this nation is omniscient and omni-powerful, like God, even though the justice system depends upon fallible men and women, and even though the system weights its scales in favor of the possibly guilty.

According to Jonathan Harr, author of *A Civil Action,* considered by many legal experts to be one of the most realistic depictions of the modern American legal system: "Truth is found at the bottom of a bottomless pit."

That sentiment is perhaps a little too cynical. Nevertheless, the fight to reach the truth is not really a balanced one. The rights afforded to defendants under the Constitution provide them with pretty heavy artillery. Prosecutors have much to contend with; that they are able to bring guilty people to justice is a testament to their work and the work of law enforcement in general. But they—and we—can do better, as the policies of the last decade have made clear. Perhaps the most important thing for the general public to reckon with is that justice is never truly impartial. She fights with one hand tied behind her back, you might say, or holding her book. When justice is slow or denied, it may be because she was not permitted to use her full might. That is the system under which we all must operate. It is the system we must all understand. It is the system that we all must, sometimes, forgive.

Index

A

A Hundred Guilty Persons, 5,
12, 13
A Living Bill of Rights
(Doubleday, 1961), 15
A.V. Jennings, 50
Abe Fortas, 19
Address at Faneuil Hall, Boston,
Massachusetts, on the 150th
anniversary of the Battle of
Bunker Hill (June 17, 1925),
40
Alan Dershowitz, 59
Alec MacGillis, 111
Alexander Hamilton, 29
Alfonso A. Narvaez, 92
Allan Blanchard, 98
Amelia McDonell-Parry, 110
American Revolution, 89
American Revolutionary War, 3,
154
Andrew Jay Graham, 137
Angela Dawson, 117, 118
Anthony Pirone, 103
Apodaca v. Oregon, 406 U.S.
404 (1972), 32
April Wolfe, 101
Aristotle, 147
Arthur McDuffie, 97
Authority of Law, 162

B

Bail, 4, 34, 35, 41, 64, 132, 138,
148

Baltimore, 74, 75, 76, 77, 78, 79,
80, 81, 82, 83, 84, 85, 86, 87,
88, 109, 110, 111, 117, 118, 119,
120, 121, 122, 123, 124, 125,
131, 132, 136, 137, 138, 139,
140, 141, 143, 146, 148, 149,
180
Baltimore City Consent Decree,
79
Baltimore Riots, 109
Barry Scheck, 59
Barry Williams, 110
Ben Schreckinger, 78
Benjamin Curtis, 7
Benjamin Franklin, 5, 13
Betts v. Brady, 316 U.S. 455
(1942), 18
Beyond a Reasonable Doubt, 13,
42, 52, 73, 90, 142, 153, 155
Bill Chappell, 114
Bill of Rights, 4, 15, 147
Black Lives Matter, 12, 112
Book of Exodus, 162
Boston Massacre of 1770, 4
Boston Tea Party of 1773, 4
Brad Polumbo, 113
Brian Rice, 110
Brian W. Rice, 83
British Monarchy, 4, 40
Broken Windows, 71, 72, 74, 75,
76, 77, 78, 80, 81, 82, 87,
102, 105, 133, 141, 149
Byron White, 43

C

C. McCormick, Evidence (1954) 13

Caesar Goodman, 110

Caldwell v. Texas, 137 U.S. 692 (1891), 11

Camden, New Jersey Riots, 92

Casey Anthony, 63, 65, 66

Certiorari, 19, 23, 28

Charles Evan Hughes, 40, 126

Charles Katz, 24

Charles-Louis de Secondat, 3

Christopher Darden, 59

Cincinnati Riots, 102

Civil Rights Movement, 13, 89

Clarence Darrow, 89

Clarence Gideon, 19

Clement Lloyd, 98

Clifford Glover, 93

Clyde Mattox, 32

Colonists, 3, 40

Consent Decree, 81, 87

Contemplation of Justice, 161

Counsel, 13, 17, 18, 19, 38, 41, 49, 120, 121, 123, 126, 147, 180

COVID-19, 111

Cruel and Unusual Punishment, 4, 35, 36, 41, 148

CSI Effect, 142, 143, 144, 145

D

Dakin Andone, 104

Dan White, 95, 96

Dana Levitz, 137

Daniel Pantaleo, 105, 109

Darrell Brooks, 117, 118

Darren Wilson, 106, 109

Darryl Gates, 100

David Childs, 102

Deborah Rhode, 11, 12

Declaration of Independence, 4

Derek Chauvin, 112, 114

DNA Evidence, 59, 61, 144, 145

Dollree Mapp, 22, 23

Donald E. Shelton, 143

Doran Johnson, 106

Double Jeopardy, 4, 147

Douglas Linder, 45, 53

Dred Scott v. Sandford, 60 U.S. 393, (1857), 7

Due Process, 4, 13, 18, 19, 39, 41, 148

Duke University, 31

E

Earl Warren, 20, 27, 31

Ed Norris, 137

Edward Nero, 83, 110

Eighth Amendment, 4, 34, 35, 36, 38, 148

Emma Bowman, 114

Emma Hernandez, 66

England, 20

English Assize Court, 31

English Common Law, 31

Equal Justice, 16, 10, 11, 12, 148, 150, 159

Equal Protection, 5, 79, 148

Eric Garner, 105, 106, 108, 111

Ernesto Miranda, 21, 22

Exclusionary Rule, 23

F

F. Lee Bailey, 56, 59

Federalist, 3, 4, 16, 29

Fifth Amendment, 4, 20, 22, 37,

41, 45, 49, 147, 153
Founding Fathers, 3, 5, 13, 15,
   67, 147, 150
Fourteenth Amendment, 4, 18,
   19, 31, 41, 53, 58, 79, 148
Fourth Amendment, 4, 22, 23,
   24, 25, 26, 27, 28, 37, 41, 147
Fraternal Order of Police, 84
Freddie Gray, 82, 109, 110
Furman v. Georgia, 408 U.S.
   238 (1972), 35, 38

G

Garrett E. Miller, 83
Gene Ryan, 84
George Floyd, 12, 111, 113, 114
George Kelling, 71, 75
George Moscone, 95
George Sutherland, 18
Gideon v. Wainwright, 372 U.S.
   335 (1963), 19, 38, 39
Grand Jury, 4, 31, 91, 106, 108,
   109, 110, 147
Gregg v. Georgia, 428 U.S. 153
   (1976), 38
Gregg v. Georgia, Proffitt v.
   Florida, Jurek v. Texas,
   Woodson v. North Carolina,
   and Roberts v. Louisiana,
   428 U.S. 153 (1976), 37
Gun Trace Task Force, 111, 131

H

Harlem Riots, 90
Harvey Milk, 95
Hearsay, 32
Houston, TX, Riots, 94

I

I can't breathe, 105, 112

Illinois v. Wardlow, 528 U.S. 119
   (2000), 26, 28, 37, 73
In re Winship, 357 U.S. 358
   (1970), 42
Insurrection, 4
Intolerable Acts of 1774, 4

J

J. Wigmore, Evidence, 2497 (3d
   ed. 1940), 13, 42
James K. Bredar, 87
James Madison, 3, 16
James Powell, 90, 112
James Wilson, 71
Janet Reno, 98
Jessica Lussenhop, 132
Jill Carter, 78
Jim Crow, 31, 32
Johannes Mehserle, 103
John Adams, 16
John G. Roberts, Jr., 71
John Gramlich, 87
John Legend, 157, 158, 159
John Marshall, 16, 161
John Stephens, 157, 158
John Terry, 27
Johnnie Cochran, 59
Jon Carson, 157, 158, 159
Jonathan Harr, 163
Jose Campos Torres, 94
Jose Morales, 138
Joseph Conforti, 51
Joseph F. Murphy, 137
Jurek v. Texas, 428 U.S. 262
   (1976), 38
Jury, 4, 13, 29, 30, 31, 32, 33, 35,
   36, 38, 41, 42, 50, 51, 52, 55,
   56, 59, 60, 62, 63, 65, 66, 80,
   91, 94, 96, 98, 99, 100, 101,
   103, 104, 106, 108, 110, 120,

121, 122, 123, 140, 141, 142, 143, 145, 146, 147, 148, 149, 155

Justice Without a Blindfold, 161

Justin George, 85

Justine Barron, 110

K

Katz v. United States, 389 U.S. 347 (1967), 24, 37

Kenneth Ravenell, 136, 139

Kevin Clark, 132

King George, 3, 147

King George III, 3

Klopfer v. North Carolina, 386 U.S. 213 (1967), 30, 38, 39

L

Lady Justice, 160

Larry Hogan, 84

Laura Shackel, 58

Laurie Wills, 118

Life, Liberty, and Property, 4, 148

Lizzie Borden, 45, 51, 55, 153

Long, Hot Summer of 1967, 91

Loretta Lynch, 84

Los Angeles Police Department, 62

Los Angeles Riots, 99

Lou Cannon, 99, 100

Louis Brandeis, 129

M

Magna Carta, 31

Majesty of Justice, 161

Majesty of Law, 162

Mapp v. Ohio, 367 U.S. 643 (1961), 22, 37, 39, 69

Marbury v. Madison, 5 U.S. 137 (1803), 15

Marcia Clark, 59

Marilyn Mosby, 83, 109, 149

Marlena Baldacci, 104

Martin Chambers, 92, 112

Martin McFadden, 27

Martin O'Malley, 75, 79, 88

Martin Stezano, 95

Matthew Clarke, 134

Mattox v. United States, 156 U.S. 237 (1895), 32, 38

Merriam-Webster's Dictionary, 10, 150, 153

Miami Riots, 97, 98

Michael Brown, 83, 106, 108, 112

Michael Steele, 78

Michelle Ye Hee Lee, 77

Miranda v. Arizona, 384 U.S. 436 (1966), 20, 37

Miranda Warnings, 13

Mirandized, 13

Momodu Gondo, 132

Moody Park Riot of 1978, 94

Moses, 162

Mount Sinai, 162

N

NAACP, 18

Nathan Braverman, 80

National Guard, 84, 92

New York City Riots, 104

Nicholas St. Fleur, 105

Nicole Brown Simpson, 58, 60, 62

O

O.J. Simpson, 58, 153

Oakland Riots, 103

Oliver Wendell Holmes, 5, 9, 10, 16, 131
Olmstead v. United States, 277 U.S. 428 (1928), 25, 129
Operation Hammer, 102
Orange County Sheriff's Department, 64
Oscar Grant, 103, 104

P

Page Croyder, 124
Patrick Henry, 4
Paul Guzzo,, 91
Peter Klopfer, 31
Potter Stewart, 25
Powell v. Alabama, 287 U.S. 45 (1932), 17, 38, 39
Power of Government, 162
Privacy Clause, 23
Probable Cause, 4, 22, 26, 72
Proffitt v. Florida, 428 U.S. 242 (1976), 38

Q

Queens, New York Riots, 93

R

Rafael Rodriguez Gonzalez, 92
Ramos v. Louisiana, 140 S. Ct. 1390, 206 L.Ed.2d 583 (2020), 32
Reasonable and Articulable Suspicion, 73
Reginald Denny, 101
Research Past, 161, 162
Richard Byrd, 139
Richard Chilton, 27
Richard Kennedy, 9, 10
Right to Counsel, 17

Robert H. Jackson, 135
Robert Kardashian, 59
Robert Long, 138
Robert Longley, 87
Roberts v. Louisiana, 428 U.S. 325 (1976), 38
Rodney King, 62, 99
Roger Owensby, Jr., 102
Roger W. Titus, 137
Rudy Giuliani, 74, 75, 76
Ryan Spence, 102

S

Sam Sheppard, 53, 58, 59
San Francisco, CA, Riots, 95
Sandra Bland, 84
Sandra Day O'Connor, 116
Scottsboro Boys, 17
Scroll of Law, 162
Searches and Seizures, 4, 22, 24, 37, 147
Self-Incrimination, 4, 20, 37, 45, 49, 121, 147
Separation of Powers, 3
Sixth Amendment, 4, 17, 18, 19, 29, 30, 31, 32, 33, 38, 41, 53, 58, 63, 77, 147
Smithsonian Magazine, 51
Sonia Sotomayor, 156
Speedy and Public Trial, 4, 41, 147
Speedy Trial, 31, 32, 41, 117, 120, 121, 122, 127, 148
Spirit of the Law, 3
Stacey Koon, 100
Stack v. Boyle, 342 U.S. 1 (1951), 38
Stamp Act of 1765, 4
Stanley Needleman, 136, 137, 139

Stare Decisis, 13
Statue of Liberty, 163
Stephanie Condon, 79, 88
Stephen Roach, 102
Stonewall Riots, 96

T

Tampa Race Riots, 91
Ted Prudente, 149
Ten Commandments, 162
Terry Stop, 26, 28
Terry v. Ohio, 392 U.S. 1 (1968),
    26, 37, 73
Terry W. Denson, 94
The Book of Judgment, 161
The Federalist Papers, 3, 4
The Missouri Riots, 106
The Spirit of Justice, 161
The Works of Benjamin Franklin
    Vol. XI (John Bigelow ed.,
    Fed. Ed. 1904), 13
Thomas Allers, 133
Thomas Gilligan, 91
Thomas Jefferson, 4, 16
Thomas Shea, 94
Tim Ott, 63
Timothy Thomas, 102
Tom Bradley, 100
Tom Clark, 23
Totality of the Circumstances,
    73
Townshend Acts of 1767, 4
Trayvon Martin, 83
"Twinkie" Defense, 96
Tyranny, 3, 5, 30, 154

U

United States v. Salerno, 481
    U.S. 739 (1987), 34, 38

United States v. Wade, 388 U.S.
    218 (1967), 43
University of Maryland School
    of Law, 74, 119

V

Vera Institute of Justice, 87, 88

W

War Room, 118, 119, 124, 125,
    127, 145
Watts v. Indiana, 228 U.S. 49
    (1949), 135
Wayne Jenkins, 132
Weeks v. United States, 232 U.S.
    383 (1914), 37
Westminster Statute, 163
White Night Riots, 95, 96
William Bratton, 76
William Brennan, 36
William Clinton, 98
William Furman, 35
William H. "Billy" Murphy, 138
William Hodgman, 59
William Lozano, 98
William O. Douglas, 15
William Porter, 110
William Purpura, 137
William Rehnquist, 28
Wolf v. Colorado, 338 U.S. 25
    (1949), 23
Woodson v. North Carolina, 428
    U.S. 280 (1976), 38
World Justice Project, 151, 152
Writ of Mandamus, 16

Acknowledgments

To all who have had an overwhelmingly positive influence on my life, specifically:

• First and foremost, I would like to thank God for the opportunities I have had in my life and for watching out for and blessing me.

• Wendy Oberer — Thank you for being the most amazing woman on the planet and the love of my life.

• Zach Oberer — Thank you for being the most amazing son and the most talented member of our family.

• Mom and Dad — I appreciate everything you did for me, the effort you put into me, and the love and dedication shown in raising me. Although you are not here anymore, I still strive to make you proud every day. Thanks for everything.

• Mary Lou Fetzer (Grandma) and Irvin "Bud" Fetzer (Grandpa) — I appreciate you being the best people I have ever known. Thank you for also being the best grandparents anyone could ever have.

• Sonia Maldonado — Thank you for being you—which I would describe as simply an amazing and fantastic person and one of the best people to walk the earth.

• John Melendez — Thank you for being a true leader of people and for finding a way to make everyone around you reach their full potential.

• Carlos Hernandez — Thank you for being one of the planet's all-time best leaders and a personal hero of mine.

• Doug Free — Thank you for teaching me how to get after it. I would not be where I am today had it not been for you.

• Michael Dixon — Thank you for teaching me how to surmount insurmountable obstacles. I would not be here today had it not been for you.

• John DeBrizzi — Thank you for being the genius to push me to be my best with so many different approaches...you are brilliant.

• Althea Handy — Thank you for being one of the shiniest gems of the U.S. judiciary.

• Bill O'Connell — Thank you for being truly inspirational and a living, breathing example of a fully developed human being.

• Paul Rieger — Thank you for your brilliance, support, and always perfectly timed humor.

• Donald Gifford — Thank you for being one of the very best law professors in the United States. Thank you for being not just a talented and motivating professor, but for possessing so many intangible qualities and traits that truly set you apart from nearly everyone. It was humbling to learn from the best.

• David Kochanski — Thank you for being an amazing lawyer and an even more amazing person.

• Marilyn Ettinger — Thank you for your support, encouragement, judgment, and belief in me.

• Jack Egan — Thank you for your leadership and insight into things I would have never known had I not known you.

• Ann McGovern — Thank you for the lessons you taught me and for always sticking with your convictions, even if that meant tough love was required.

• Mark Teague — Thank you for being an amazing human being, for your support through my growing pains, and for being one of my all-time heroes and role models.

• Springfield South High School (now Springfield High School) — To all the fine educators who find a way to not only educate but also dedicate their lives to advancing talented students from humble beginnings—particularly Mr. "Doc" Willets, Mrs. Maloney, Mrs. Tittle, among many others...thank you!

• New Jersey City University — I have never seen such an amazing hidden gem as this institution. Thank you for admitting me and for all the opportunities you provided. Overflowing with educators and administrators who truly care, I have never personally seen an institution that not only educates at a high level but also develops and brings out the very maximum ability in its students.

• University of Maryland Francis King Carey School of Law — Thank you for a second-to-none legal education at the highest level. Thank you for teaching me to think outside the box, critically, and in ways that differ from how I was wired. Understanding the law can be developed from books, but learning how to "think" takes special instruction, dedication, and care from the faculty to each student. Thank you for honing this ability in me. I feel fortunate to have been able to attend the third-oldest law school in the United States. Thank you for admitting me.

About Atmosphere Press

Atmosphere Press is an independent, full-service publisher of excellent books in all genres and for all audiences. Learn more about what we do at atmospherepress.com.

We encourage you to check out some of Atmosphere's latest releases, which are available at Amazon.com and via order from your local bookstore:

Finding Us, by Kristin Rehkamp

The Ideological and Political System of Banselism, by Royard Halmonet Vantion (Ancheng Wang)

Unconditional: Loving and Losing an Addict, by Lizzy and Adam

Telling Tales and Sharing Secrets, by Jackie Collins, Diana Kinared, and Sally Showalter

Nursing Homes: A Missionary's Journey Through Heaven's Waiting Room, by Tim Eatman Ph.D.

Timeline of Stars, by Joe Adcock

A Boy Who Loved Me, by Wilson Semitti

The Injustice in Justice, by Charmaine Loverin

Living in the Gray, by Katie Weber

Living with Veracity, Dying with Dignity, by Alison Clay-Duboff

Noah's Rejects, by Rob Kagan

A lot of Questions (with no answers)?, by Jordan Neben

Cowboy from Prague: An Immigrant's Pursuit of the American Dream, by Charles Ota Heller

Sleeping Under the Bridge, by Melissa Baker

The Only Prayer I Ever Have to Say Is Thank You, by M. Kaya Hill

Amygdala Blue, by Paul Lomax

A Caregiver's Love Story, by Nancie Wiseman Attwater

About the Author

ERIC D. OBERER is a former Baltimore, Maryland prosecutor who has spent his career working as a civil litigator, trial lawyer, title attorney, land development and acquisition negotiator at a major law firm, and in-house counsel to a Fortune 500 company. He spent much of his early career around national policymakers, working as a law clerk for the U.S. House of Representatives Committee on Small Business and the U.S. Army Judge Advocate General's (JAG) Corps for the First Infantry Division in Germany, as well as a White House intern, United Nations intern, and page for the United States Congress.

Eric received his Juris Doctorate from the University of Maryland Francis King Carey School of Law and a Bachelor of Science in finance from New Jersey City University, where he was president of his class and named the Thomas M. Gerrity Scholar-Athlete of the Year for NCAA tennis. Eric currently serves as a member of the board of directors of the Maryland Land Title Association and chairs its underwriter section as well as the committee on education. He also chairs a committee within the Maryland State Bar Association. Eric is licensed to practice law in the State of Maryland and the District of Columbia and is a member of both the Maryland and Washington, D.C. Bar Associations.